THE BATTLE FOR AFGHANISTAN

Following the terrorist attacks on America on 9/11, British and US forces entered Afghanistan and backed the Northern Alliance to eject the Taliban and al-Qaeda from Kabul. NATO quickly took responsibility for security in the capital, but a hardcore of Taliban fighters opposed the Western troops. British and US forces mounted a hunt in the Tora Bora Mountains for Osama bin Laden, the terrorist leader behind the attacks on America, but he had fled.

During the operation, attacks on multi-national coalition troops slowly increased. Multi-national troops now took responsibility for security and development in regions across the country which had been under years of repression with first the Soviets and then the Taliban. By 2006, UK forces faced increasing hostility in Helmand as insurgents swarmed in from Pakistan. In response, Washington surged US forces into the country. However, by 2010 the UK and US were making plans to pass command and control of the country to Afghan forces. And, in 2014 combat operations in southern Afghanistan and much of the rest of the country ended. A 'train and advise' capability, headed by the US and supported

by international troops remained in Kabul to mentor the Afghan National Army, which was equipped with the latest weapons and equipment. In late 2020, the then President Donald Trump had announced that US forces would be leaving in early 2021 and after the election the new administration of President Joe Biden reviewed the decision and gave a new timeline of September 11, 2021 – the 20th anniversary of the attacks on the United States - for all troops to be out.

Unfortunately, the Taliban saw the Western withdrawal as their chance and marched on Kabul seizing provinces as they advanced. The Afghan National Army, which the Coalition had spent 20 years training and equipping, collapsed with most of the weapons and equipment falling in to the hands of the Taliban. The insurgents moved into Kabul as the Afghan President fled, sparking panic, and forcing the biggest international air evacuation since World War Two. In total, over 122,000 people were airlifted out of the country.

The evacuation was completed on August 30, 2021, one day before a deadline agreed on with the Taliban. The conflict cost the lives of more than 3,000 coalition personnel with another 112,000 wounded. In addition, an estimated 83,000 Afghan nationals and insurgents died. This special publication is intended to mark the anniversary of the departure from the country and contains personal accounts from UK and US soldiers, profiles some of the main events, and illustrates the story with many never seen before pictures.

David Reynolds Editor

CONTENTS

03 Introduction

06 First into Action
The terror attacks on America in September 2001, left a nation grieving as the country's armed forces stood poised to be first into action. Almost 3,000 people lay dead.

18 Security and Stability
In mid-2002, President Bush was briefed that the initial battle for Afghanistan was over. But the struggle for peace was to prove much harder than ejecting the Taliban from Kabul.

30 Baptism of Fire
In 2006, the coalition International Security Assistance Force (ISAF) main focus was on Helmand in southern Afghanistan. Here British troops were to deploy in the spring as part of NATO's (ISAF) stage three delivery of security and reconstruction.

40 Fighting Explodes
In 2007, insurgents stepped up their offensive across the country from Gardez in the east to Kunduz in the north, as well as Uruzgan and Helmand further south. The improvised explosive device IED was now the Taliban's weapon of choice.

50 The Surge – More Troops
Political pressure to send more troops to Afghanistan had been constant since the arrival of international troops in the country. Commanders faced the dilemma of taking ground from the Taliban, but not being able to hold it because of a lack of soldiers.

62 The Hunt for Bin Laden
In August 2010, US intelligence agencies obtained information that indicated that Osama bin Laden was living in a compound in northern Pakistan. America's 'most wanted' was now the subject of a top-secret plan.

76 The Afghan National Army
Delivering a formed Afghan Army was seen as a priority to ensure that the government took control of its national defence policy and allow international forces to leave.

86 End of Combat Operations
In 2009 President Obama said his goal was to start withdrawing American personnel by 2011. The following year, UK Prime Minister David Cameron suggested all British forces would be withdrawn by 2015.

96 Taliban Resurgence
The Taliban's approach to the coalition intervention in Afghanistan was patient anger, they knew their time would come – the insurgents were in no rush. When the ISAF began withdrawing, the insurgents filled the void.

106 Kabul Evacuation
In 2021, Kabul was the scene of the biggest evacuation since the Berlin airlift following World War Two. As the Taliban marched on the city there were fears of a bloodbath in the capital.

ISBN: 978 1 83632 004 3
Editor: David Reynolds
Senior editor, specials: Roger Mortimer
Email: roger.mortimer@keypublishing.com
Cover Design: Steve Donovan
Design: SJmagic DESIGN SERVICES, India
Advertising Sales Manager: Sam Clark
Email: sam.clark@keypublishing.com
Tel: 01780 755131
Advertising Production: Becky Antoniades
Email: Rebecca.antoniades@keypublishing.com

SUBSCRIPTION/MAIL ORDER
Key Publishing Ltd, PO Box 300,
Stamford, Lincs,
PE9 1NA
Tel: 01780 480404
Subscriptions email:
subs@keypublishing.com

Mail Order email: orders@keypublishing.com
Website: www.keypublishing.com/shop

PUBLISHING
Group CEO and Publisher: Adrian Cox

Published by
Key Publishing Ltd, PO Box 100,
Stamford, Lincs, PE9 1XQ
Tel: 01780 755131
Website: www.keypublishing.com

PRINTING
Precision Colour Printing Ltd, Haldane,
Halesfield 1, Telford, Shropshire. TF7 4QQ

DISTRIBUTION
Seymour Distribution Ltd, 2 Poultry Avenue,
London, EC1A 9PU
Enquiries Line: 02074 294000.

We are unable to guarantee the bona fides of any of our advertisers. Readers are strongly recommended to take their own precautions before parting with any information or item of value, including, but not limited to money, manuscripts, photographs, or personal information in response to any advertisements within this publication.

© Key Publishing Ltd 2024
All rights reserved. No part of this magazine may be reproduced or transmitted in any form by any means, electronic or mechanical, including photocopying, recording or by any information storage and retrieval system, without prior permission in writing from the copyright owner. Multiple copying of the contents of the magazine without prior written approval is not permitted.

CHAPTER ONE

FIRST INTO ACTION

The terror attacks on America in September 2001 left a nation grieving and its armed forces anxious to strike back. The attacks on September 11, 2001 left almost 3,000 people dead, after Osama bin Laden's cohorts in al-Qaeda hijacked four commercial airplanes, deliberately crashing two of them into the upper floors of the North and South Towers of the World Trade Centre complex and a third plane into the Pentagon in Arlington, Virginia. Passengers on the fourth hijacked plane, Flight 93, fought back, and the plane was crashed into an empty field in western Pennsylvania about 20 minutes by air from Washington. As well as the 19 hijackers, the attacks killed 2,977 innocent people: 2,753 in New York; 184 people were killed at the Pentagon; and 40 more were killed on Flight 93. Within days the country's commander in chief, President George W Bush, placed his military at high readiness and directed them to 'prepare for combat operations'. The man that had approved the savage suicide attacks was a wealthy Saudi called Osama bin Laden who created the terror group al-Qaeda. His right-hand man

In one of the first actions of the war, US special forces were flown into northern Afghanistan aboard MH-47 Chinook helicopters to meet up with the Northern Alliance. (DPL)

and architect of the attacks was Khalid Sheikh Mohammed, an engineer with a deep hatred of the United States. He had been involved in the 1993 bombing of the World Trade Centre in New York and was alleged to be the 'brains' behind 9/11. Washington and its allies quickly forged a coalition ready to fight back in a global offensive, which President Bush termed the 'war on terror'. Bin Laden and al-Qaeda had trained and planned their attack on the United States from Afghanistan. They were now hiding in northern Afghanistan, where the group had forged links with the Taliban - an organisation which in 2001 ruled most of the central and southern area of the country with an iron fist, imposing Sharia law across communities.

On October 7, just a month after the atrocities, President George Bush addressed the nation from the White House in what became known as his 'war on terror' speech. In it he warned that al-Qaeda and the Taliban were about to pay a price for their evil attacks. The terrorists who attacked the United States had been trained at remote camps in Afghanistan, facilitated by the Taliban and as Bush spoke, the battle for Afghanistan commenced. The

The terrorist attacks on America in September 2001 left a nation grieving and its armed forces poised to retaliate. (US DoD)

mission, codenamed Operation Enduring Freedom was launched with airstrikes by US bombers and Tomahawk cruise missiles launched from US fighter aircraft and two Royal Navy nuclear submarines on station in the Indian Ocean.

Northern Alliance

As part of the President's plan to hit back at the attackers, US special forces flew into the north of Afghanistan to rendezvous with the Northern Alliance, a group heavily opposed to the Taliban. On October 19, 2001, a 12 strong team from the 5th Special Forces Group's Operational Detachment Alpha 595 (ODA 595) were inserted into Afghanistan in a MH-47 Chinook helicopter to rendezvous with General Abdul Rashid Dostum and his Uzbek militia to help them liberate the region from the Taliban. Dostum was a former communist general who had earned a 'colourful' reputation as a tough commander, he had little patience and a strong stomach for combat. The plan was for the coalition troops to advance south, with the Northern Alliance, and eject the Taliban from Kabul - a distance of almost 280 miles across mountains and valleys, much of which was held by warlords, loyal to the Taliban, and in the pay of al-Qaeda. The US soldiers carried little equipment and were offered horses to ride alongside their mounted hosts. However, the saddles and riding gear weren't designed to accommodate the Americans, who were larger and heavier than their Afghan counterparts and quite a bit of tack had to be adapted for their larger frames. Broken stirrups had to be repaired with parachute cargo straps. However, the horses allowed them to move at any time of day or night, in all terrains, and all weathers. Meanwhile, the Taliban and al-Qaeda had limited mobility, but they had armoured vehicles and tanks which the Soviet Army had left behind when they exited Afghanistan in 1989. ODA 595 had the capability to direct coalition bombers to strike the heavily armed enemy. ODA 595 was one of a number of special forces units, including Delta teams, sent into Afghanistan to help the Northern

CHAPTER ONE

Royal Navy nuclear powered hunter killer submarines launched Tomahawk cruise missiles at al-Qaeda training camps inside Afghanistan. (UK MoD)

USAF bombers targeting the Taliban and anti-coalition militia were directed onto their targets by coalition special forces. (DPL)

Alliance eject the Taliban from power after the 9/11 attacks. Five out of the 12 men were combat veterans who had served in Somalia, Bosnia, or the first Gulf War, their average age was 32. To learn about the country the team read National Geographic magazines, tourist maps, and scanned the internet to study the region. Specifically, they wanted to identify the anti-Taliban leaders of the Tajiks, Uzbeks, and Hazaras who ultimately formed the Northern Alliance. The Green Berets and CIA counterparts worked to unite these groups to form a militia of nearly 5,000 fighters.

On November 10, 2001 after a three-day bloody fight with the Taliban, ODA 595 and the Northern Alliance liberated the city of Mazar-e-Sharif. More than 4,000 Taliban fighters had headed for Mazar with the intention of releasing prisoners. On November 7 and 8, US aircraft had bombed Taliban positions and then on November 9, the combined force of ODA595 and Northern Alliance entered Mazar and fought a major battle against the Taliban at a fortress called Qala-i-Jangi, which was being used as the prison. More than 400 inmates escaped and gained arms from Taliban fighters in the area and launched an assault on western forces. An unknown number of coalition soldiers were injured including a CIA operative subsequently named Johnny Micheal Spann,

Northern Alliance vehicles joined the advance north of Kabul. The missiles mounted on their vehicle were taken from a captured Russian helicopter during the war with the Soviets. (Yves Debay/DPL)

Northern Alliance fighters pause during the fighting to remove the Taliban from power. (US DoD)

The US troops inserted into Afghanistan had no vehicles and opted to ride to war on horses, a skill that has now become part of special forces training. (US DoD)

who was mortally wounded and became the first US combat casualty of the war. Spann, a former US Marine was a CIA operator attached to US forces. He had detained an inmate called John Walker Lindh, who claimed he was Irish but was in fact an American citizen. Spann and other CIA officers were questioning prisoners when Spann became separated and surrounded by angry inmates who attacked him. His colleague Dave Tyson shot several prisoners before seeing that Spann was dead. Tyson killed dozens of fighters as he fought his way into the northern half of the fort where US force was. John Walker Lindh was detained, he had been fighting with the insurgents. He was extradited to the United States where he stood trial in February 2002 and was sentenced to 20 years imprisonment.

On November 13, 2001, the Northern Alliance marched into Kabul having fought their way to the city. Within days of the liberation, people started to listen to music, which had been banned by the Taliban. Kabul radio was back in action and for the first time ➲

DON'T MISS OUT ON OTHER KEY MILITARY MAGAZINE SPECIALS
If you'd like information about Key Publishing's military books, magazine specials, subscription offers and the latest product releases sent directly to your inbox. **Scan here »**

CHAPTER ONE

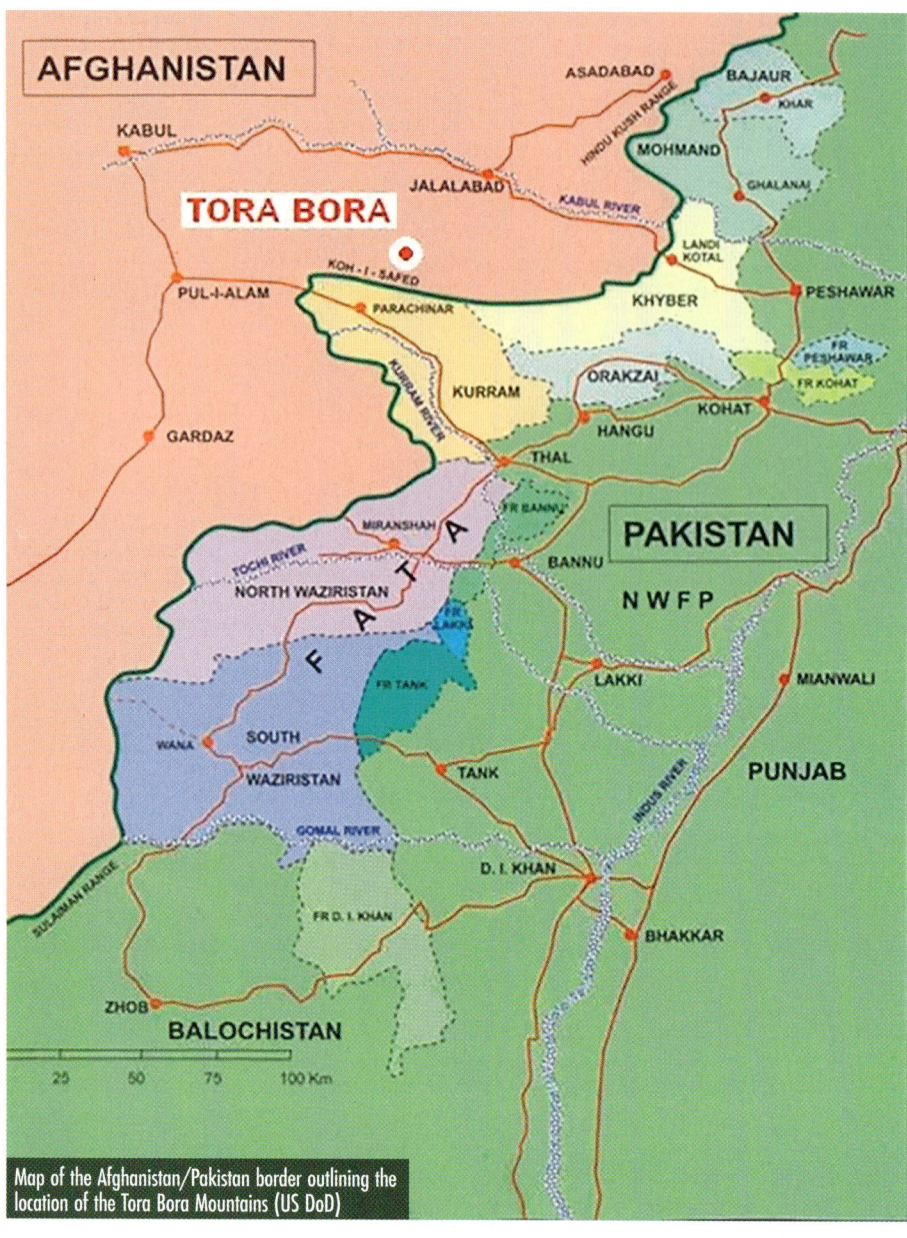

Map of the Afghanistan/Pakistan border outlining the location of the Tora Bora Mountains (US DoD)

in five years men queued at barbers' shops to have their beards shaved off.

Later the liberators moved to Bagram airfield, a large, remote base an hour's journey north of Kabul. Here, just months after the terror attacks on the US, Western forces breathed new life into the decaying buildings and turned it into the main operating base for the coalition from which to hunt Osama bin Laden and his cohorts.

Tora Bora

Meanwhile, the Taliban had fled Kabul in the wake of the arrival of the Northern Alliance and re-grouped at their spiritual home of Kandahar. The US mounted an operation to 'kill or capture' and hundreds of fighters were cornered at the airfield in a firefight which became known as the 'Taliban's last stand', many were killed or wounded, while others surrendered. Those who escaped headed south into Helmand Province – a region that had seen little coalition presence apart from US and French special forces patrols. US and coalition intelligence officers now presented evidence that Osama bin Laden (OBL) and his al-Qaeda fighters had fled to the Tora Bora mountains, southeast of Kabul. On November 30, 2001, a coalition of US special forces, Joint Special Operations Command soldiers, and a detachment of CIA operatives codenamed 'Jawbreaker' and led by Gary Berntsen, joined forces with Afghan tribal militias, and began to call in airstrikes on the al-Qaeda training camp. The Battle of Tora Bora had begun.

Ever since the September 11 attacks, the CIA had been monitoring reports of bin Laden's movements. Earlier, on November 10, he had been spotted near Jalalabad while traveling in a convoy of 200 pick-up trucks in the direction of a training camp in the Tora Bora mountains. The US military had expected him to make a last stand there, but OBL had other plans.

Guided by locals that knew the terrain, the Americans climbed the mountains and

US Special Forces Combat Applications Group (Delta Force) disguised as Afghan civilians at Tora Bora pause for a group picture. (US DoD)

US special forces troops used pack animals to carry equipment across the mountains as they advanced with members of the Northern Alliance during the early days of operations in Afghanistan. (US DoD)

valuable intelligence, including hearing the voice of bin Laden himself. The Delta Force officer in charge, codename 'Dalton Fury' said that he was in 'no doubt' that it was OBL, and a CIA operative named Jalal, who had spent seven years studying OBL's voice signature, also confirmed it was the al-Qaeda leader.

The bunker that OBL was believed to be hiding in on December 9, had been evacuated the previous day. On December 10, the Delta Force team intercepted radio communications indicating that bin Laden was on the move, perhaps attempting to break-out. In the evening, more communications revealed OBL's location just 10km away. However, Delta Force couldn't act on this opportunity as they were engaged in a fierce firefight with other al-Qaeda fighters. On December 12, al-Qaeda forces, facing defeat, negotiated a truce with a local Afghan militia commander to give them time to surrender their weapons. In retrospect, however, some critics believe that the truce was a deception to allow a small team of al-Qaeda figures to slip away from the mountains and into Pakistan. Berntsen was furious when he heard the news of the ceasefire. He didn't trust the al-Qaeda fighters and was suspicious of their intentions to surrender. He grabbed his phone and screamed: "No cease-fire! No negotiation! We continue airstrikes!" The fighting and bombing continued but all signs of OBL had ⊃

after a few days arrived close to the training camp where OBL had been spotted early in November. Hundreds of al-Qaeda fighters were still there, heavily armed, and ready for another fight. Berntsen made a request for a battalion of 800 US Army Rangers to be flown forward. His plan was to deploy them into the mountain passes bordering Pakistan and create a 'blocking force' to cut off OBL's escape but the request was denied.

On December 3, the US special forces teams, equipped with laser-designators, called in USAF aircraft who dropped laser guided bombs to target the fighters in a 72-hour operation. The al-Qaeda fighters withdrew to higher fortified positions and dug in for the battle. On December 8, a Delta Force team in 'plain clothes' – wearing traditional Afghan clothing, having grown beards, and carrying the same weapon types as the Afghan militias - moved in on the enemy positions. They had recovered a radio from an al-Qaeda fighter, and it allowed them to eavesdrop on the enemy and gain some

Members of the Northern Alliance take a break on the advance to Kabul. (DPL)

A CH-47 helicopter drops off US special operations soldiers into the Tora Bora mountains during the mission to find Osama bin Laden. (US DoD)

CHAPTER ONE

British Royal Marine Commandos are recovered by a Chinook in the border mountains with Pakistan during follow up operations to find Osama bin Laden. (UK MoD)

British troops drive through a wadi during operations in the mountains close to the Pakistan border. (DPL)

The commandos flew over the mountain range of the Hindu Kush on their way from Bagram to the Pakistan border. (UK MoD)

evaporated. Dalton Fury later expressed regret about the failure to capitalise on this situation, feeling that he had let down his country in its time of need, and Berntsen alleged that the failure to deploy the Rangers at Tora Bora and overreliance on the Afghan militias had allowed bin Laden to escape.

Chasing Ghosts – Op Anaconda

Special Forces commanders reported that OBL had fled, but politicians and senior generals were convinced that the fugitive could still be hiding in the mountains. They ignored advice that they were chasing a ghost and now planned to send US and UK troops to search the Tora Bora region. By late 2001 politicians looked to the Bonn Agreement

Chinook helicopters operated in extreme weather to deploy and recover troops in the mountains. (US DoD)

Soldiers from the 10th Mountain Division board a Chinook in the Tora Bora mountains. (DPL)

A propaganda poster in support of Osama bin Laden found in the caves of the Tora Bora mountains. (UK MoD)

A Royal Marine passes the remains of a Soviet helicopter high in the mountains near the Pakistan border. (UK MoD)

to sanction the deployment in Afghanistan of an International Security Assistance Force (ISAF). This was a United Nations authorised force established at the request of Afghan authorities. The country lacked any credible national army or police force, and ISAF was seen as essential to dealing with a looming security vacuum in rural areas.

On December 22, 2001, Hamid Karzai's new Afghan administration was established in Kabul. In the same week, the UK announced that troops from 40 Commando Royal Marines, who had been on exercise in Oman, were to be re-deployed to Bagram. It was unclear what their role would be, but suddenly there was a rush to get more troops into the base. In early 2002, the US 10th Mountain Division and the UK's 45 Commando Royal Marines, a specialist mountain and arctic warfare cadre, were now deployed

Soldiers of the 10th Mountain Division pictured at dusk in the Tora Bora mountains. (US DoD)

CHAPTER ONE

An aerial view of Kabul, the capital of Afghanistan, located in the eastern half of the country. (DPL)

to Bagram in readiness to join the hunt for bin Laden.

During the Soviet occupation, Bagram had been a strategic base for the Russians and had also been the point of mass evacuation when they left. The American and British troops who arrived, more than a decade after Moscow's departure, found numerous reminders of the Red Army at the base. Crashed planes, bombed armoured vehicles and hundreds of Russian military tunic buttons and badges lying in the sand.

The US military organisation was impressive; in a matter of weeks handbooks on

The remnants of Soviet fighter jets which littered Kabul airport when the northern Alliance and coalition force arrived. (DPL)

US soldiers from the 101st Airborne join the hunt for Osama bin Laden in the Tora Bora mountains. (US DoD)

British paratroopers were sent to Kabul to spearhead ISAF's security and stabilisation commitment. They arrived in late December 2001. (DPL)

Afghanistan, detailing everything from enemy forces and their weapons to details such as which were the dangerous local species of spider and how to spot land mines, had been produced and distributed. Extensive communications systems were established and pre-cooked meals flown in from a US base in Germany. Bagram was a dry and dusty place where home for the troops was a tent.

The joint force was supported by Chinook helicopters who airlifted them high over the Hindu Kush to reach their area of operations in the hunt for bin Laden. During their searches of caves deep inside the Tora Bora Mountains, the US and UK soldiers discovered hundreds of tons of explosives along with a considerable amount of other evidence of al-Qaeda's presence. But there was little sign of bin-Laden - he had, as US special forces had already advised, fled the area in late 2001.

A British paratrooper armed with a general-purpose machine gun monitors a back street in Kabul. At this stage of the operation the threat was considered low, and soldiers routinely wore berets on patrol. (DPL)

Meanwhile, hundreds of Taliban prisoners were being detained by the US at Bagram in a remote prison on the edge of the airfield, to which few people had access. Whenever prisoners were flown out for further detention and interrogation at a prison facility at Guantanamo Bay on the island of Cuba, a mortar alarm was sounded at Bagram to ensure that everyone took shelter and did not see the prisoners as they were marched to a transport aircraft and flown out of the country.

Roberts Ridge

On January 4, 2002, the US 1st Special Forces Group was deployed in Gardez when a team which included a CIA 'special activities group' came under attack. Sergeant Nathan Chapman was shot by insurgents and later died. He was the first US soldier to be killed by enemy action in the war in Afghanistan. In March 2002, the US command headquarters launched Operation Anaconda with the aim of destroying remaining the al-Qaeda and Taliban forces

CHAPTER ONE

On January 4, 2002, the US 1st Special Forces Group was deployed in Gardez when a team which included a CIA 'special activities group' came under attack. (US DoD)

in the Shat-i-Kot Valley and Arma Mountains. It was the biggest mission since the Battle of Tora Bora and involved 1,700 US troops and around 1,000 pro-government Afghan militia soldiers being flown into the region southeast of Zurmat. It was originally estimated that the enemy force was around 400 strong, it later transpired to be almost 1,400. It was during the early phase of Anaconda that the deadliest incident took place. On March 3, 2002, a special forces team of US Navy Seals of Task Force 11 were to be covertly inserted at the top of Takur Ghar mountain. However, as the two Chinooks from the 160th Special Operations Aviation Regiment, codenamed Razor 3, and Razor 4, lifted off, one experienced mechanical issues. Two replacement aircraft and a C-130 Spectre gunship carried out a reconnaissance sortie above the Takur Ghar area to check for any enemy fighters and reported the area 'all clear'.

As the first helicopter landed it came under heavy fire and as it managed to lift off Petty Officer Neil Roberts fell off the rear ramp. The pilot of the heavily damaged Chinook tried to make another landing but had little control of the aircraft and was forced to make an emergency landing away from the enemy. It was too badly damaged to fly, and the aircraft was abandoned. The second Chinook was able to land and dropped its team of SEALs – under heavy fire – and left the area of operation. The Quick Reaction Force (QRF) was now called in. It consisted of 19 US Rangers, a tactical air control party to direct close air support, and a USAF special tactics team. All the ground forces as well as the air assets were experiencing communications problems and consequently, the AC-130 was unaware that another Chinook was inbound with the QRF and left the area. Poor satellite communications resulted in the Rangers heading for the 'hot' landing site surrounded by enemy fighters. The Chinook landed into a hail of enemy fire. A second Chinook ferried the remainder of the QRF and landed at an alternate

As the first helicopter landed in Gardez it came under heavy fire and as it managed to lift off Petty Officer Neal Roberts fell from the rear ramp. (US DoD)

A second Chinook ferried the remaining of the QRF, landed at an alternate site, and joined the firefight. (US DoD)

site to join the firefight. As they came under heavy fire an Australian SAS team on a long-range reconnaissance mission with the 10th Mountain Brigade was able to co-ordinate multiple coalition air strikes onto al-Qaeda positions.

In memory of the petty officer who fell from the ramp of the Chinook and was later killed, the battle of Takur Ghar is often referred to as the battle of Roberts Ridge. In total seven US personnel were killed and 12 injured.

More nations were sending troops to Kabul to support the ISAF operation, but the Taliban began a quiet resurgence. Attacks on multi-national forces now started to rise, the honeymoon period in Kabul was over.

ISAF's initial operations

Meanwhile, in late December 2001, NATO's ISAF operation to deliver peace and stability was underway. UK troops, drawn from the 2nd Battalion the Parachute Regiment, were the first to arrive in Kabul as part of a multi-national formation commanded by the UK's Major General John McColl, and which would later include troops from 18 nations. They flew in from Oman and were the first infantry battalion on the ground.

There remained a hardcore of Taliban supporters in the city watching events unfold and the coalition unit focused its efforts on 'hearts and minds' and mounted a psychological effort to build consent and stability among the population to support ISAF's presence in the city. This centred on a proactive and skilful Information operation to inform and influence the population of the city to allow the new administration to agree to future political and security structures in accordance with the Bonn Agreement.

The battalion trained a 600-strong Afghan battalion in order to get local forces on the streets of the city. The deployment of the battalion to Kabul had seen the Parachute Regiment deliver calm, stability and security. Paratroopers wore berets, maintained a low profile within the community, and made significant progress in overseeing a return to normality. The battalion's robust tactical approach had avoided major violence, gained trust, and delivered a template of operational success. Policemen had been trained, services restored, and community engagement achieved. This allowed NATO to encourage additional members to deploy troops to the city.

However, the presence of 2 PARA had not been welcomed by elements of the Taliban who now appeared to be gaining support, perhaps through intimidation. ●

CHAPTER TWO

SECURITY AND STABILITY

In mid-2002, President Bush was briefed that the initial battle for Afghanistan was over. However, the struggle for peace was to prove much more difficult than ejecting the Taliban from Kabul. The main focus of operations was now directed towards 'security and development'.

But that mission was about to take second place as Washington signed up a small coalition to embark on a second offensive.

At Bagram airbase, north of Kabul, US Army engineers were busy inside one of the old Russian aircraft hangars. They were constructing a new planning centre. It was surrounded with barbed wire and access was only permitted with a special security pass. This top-secret planning centre was for a new mission, in Iraq. Provincial Reconstruction Teams (PRTs) which had first been deployed by the US Army in Vietnam were now adopted to identify potential reconstruction projects to re-build the Afghan

The struggle for peace was to prove much more difficult than ejecting the Taliban from Kabul. (UK MoD)

At Bagram airbase, north of Kabul, US Army engineers were busy inside one of the old Russian aircraft hangars. (UK MoD)

Germany was one of the many countries who stepped forward to support reconstruction and ended up involved in combat operations. (IASF)

infrastructure and boost the economy. These teams consisted of small military units of about 150 soldiers, which included civilian experts; their role was to focus on the reinforcement of Afghan governance and legitimacy of the government in Kabul as well as identifying and funding the development of projects. This was a challenging task as in many remote areas local warlords were in charge and had little time for the government. While local people wanted water wells and roads there was a cultural suspicion as to why westerners were offering this help. The first PRT was established by the US military at Gardez in Paktia province in November 2002 and became fully operational in February 2003. By the end of the year, seven more teams were established in Mazar-e-Sharif (UK forces), Kunduz (Germany), Bamyan (New Zealand), Parwan (United States), Herat (Italy), and Kandahar (Canada). As the United States and Britain focused their main effort in Iraq, Turkey, Romania, Germany, Spain, and

CHAPTER TWO

Australia was among the many nations who agreed to deploy peace keeping troops to support reconstruction projects in the north and east of Afghanistan. (ISAF)

Australia were among the many nations who agreed to deploy peace keeping troops into Kabul. PRTs were now being established in the north and east of Afghanistan.

Suicide Attack

A Canadian general now took command of ISAF, but the security situation in Kabul had deteriorated – soldiers were being shot at and there were intelligence concerns warning about the threat of roadside bombs. On January 28, 2004 a mobile patrol, mounted by the Rifle Volunteers, a reservist unit attached to the Royal Gurkha Rifles, was hit in a suicide bomb attack. The soldiers were travelling in an open-topped Land Rover; as it passed a taxi, the Afghan driver detonated a bomb blasting himself and the soldiers. Private Jonathan Kitulagoda was killed, and four soldiers injured in the explosion, which took place within a mile of the British base at Camp Souter. Private Kitulagoda had joined the reserves during his time as a student at Plymouth University. His death was raised in a House of Commons debate by Patrick Mercer MP, who challenged the then Prime Minister Tony Blair, about the lack of armoured protected vehicles in Kabul when it was known that the threat level was high. A memorial plaque to Private Kitulagoda was erected and remains at the British Military cemetery in Sherpur Cantonment Cemetery in Kabul. Aged 23, he was the first British soldier to be killed in Afghanistan while on operations. Earlier, three British soldiers had died in Kabul as a result of non-hostile action: Private Darren George of the Royal Anglian regiment was killed when a colleague discharged his weapon; while Sergeant Robert Busuttil of the Royal Logistic Corps died when he was shot by Corporal John Gregory during an argument at a barbecue, while off duty at their Kabul base. Gregory then turned his weapon on himself.

French troops on a routine patrol outside Kabul. Paris sent troops to help train and assist the Afghans and deliver security across the country. (ISAF)

In August, the then UK Defence Secretary, Geoff Hoon MP, announced the United Kingdom would deploy six Harrier GR7 aircraft to Kandahar for an initial period of nine months. (DPL)

Private Jonathan Kitulagoda was the first British soldier to be killed in action in Kabul - four soldiers were injured in the explosion, which took place within a mile of the British base in Kabul. (DPL)

By mid-2004 the US military had approval from the Pentagon to increase the military resources at Bagram, Kandahar, and Kabul. In August, the then UK Defence Secretary, Geoff Hoon MP, announced the United Kingdom would deploy six Harrier GR7 aircraft to Kandahar for an initial period of nine-months.

In October 2004, British Army Lance Corporal Steven Sherwood, serving with the 1st Battalion Royal Gloucestershire, Berkshire, and Wiltshire Light Infantry (1 RGBWLI), was killed in Mazar-e -Sharif. He had been supporting the PRT operation in the area when his convoy was ambushed near the one-thousand-year-old Sultan Ahmed Mosque, otherwise known as the Blue Mosque. He was the second UK soldier to be killed on duty since British forces had arrived.

The Afghan Presidential elections in 2004 were held to replace the transitional government with an elected administration. Hamid Karzai was re-elected, on a platform that promised reform, security, and stability across Afghanistan. However, the security situation in Kabul and Kandahar continued to deteriorate, with violence now increasing. Airfields at both locations were coming under regular rocket attack, and by the end of the year ISAF troops in Kabul were wearing helmets and traveling in armoured vehicles. Then, three-weeks after the Afghan election and days before the US election, America's most wanted terrorist,

Osama bin Laden was now the focus of a manhunt into the Tora Bora mountains. (US DoD)

CHAPTER TWO

Canadian soldiers joined the mission into the mountains. (US DoD)

Osama bin Laden, released a videotaped message in which he taunted the Bush administration and admitted responsibility for the attacks on September 11, 2001.

Operation Red Wings

In June 2005, US forces mounted an operation to clear Taliban and anti-coalition forces (ACM) from Kunar province in northeastern Afghanistan, which bordered Pakistan. In removing Taliban and ACM from the area the mission supported ISAF's aim of delivering stability to the east of the country. The plan was for a US Navy SEAL reconnaissance team to insert into the region and identify the militant leader, Ahmad Shah. Shah was a ruthless warlord and criminal who had a force of more than 200 under his command. A direct-action team would insert by MH-47 helicopter and be followed by US Marines who would kill or capture Shah and his men. The follow-on aim would be a focus on security and stabilisation in the area. Late in the night of June 27, 2005, two Chinook MH-47 approached Sawtalo Sar, a mountain almost 10,000ft high in the Hindu Kush. As one Chinook made a number of 'decoy drops' to mislead any Taliban observers, the other inserted a four-man SEAL team in an area just to south of the feature. The team - Lieutenant Michael P Murphy, Petty Officer Danny Dietz, Petty Officer Matthew G Axelson, and medic Marcus Luttrell - moved to a pre-determined location but were compromised by local goatherders. Murphy decided to release them as they were civilians rather than combatants, but the team knew that the goatherders would inform the Taliban and so moved to a fallback position from where they planned to call for a helicopter extraction. However, within an hour, the team was attacked by Shah and his men who were armed with machine guns and rocket propelled grenades. The fighting was intense as the insurgents also called up 82mm mortars and moved heavy machine guns into position. The SEAL team were forced into the northeast gulch of Sawtalo Sar, on the Shuryek Valley side of the mountain. Despite the intensity of the firefight and suffering grave gunshot wounds himself, Murphy is credited with risking his own life to save the lives of his teammates. Intent on contacting headquarters but realising this would be impossible in the extreme terrain where they were fighting, with complete disregard for his own life Murphy moved into the open, where he could gain a better position to transmit a call to get help for his men. Moving away from the protective mountain rocks, he knowingly exposed himself to increased enemy gunfire. This deliberate and heroic act deprived him of cover and made him a target for the enemy. While continuing to be fired upon, Murphy contacted the SOF Quick Reaction Force at Bagram Air Base and requested assistance.

Seal operator Dany Dietz also died in the Red Wings mission in Kunar Province. (US DoD)

The plan was for a US Navy SEAL reconnaissance team to insert into the region and identify the militant leader, Ahmad Shah. (DPL)

Lt Michael Murphy (left) with Petty Officer Matthew Axelson. Both were killed in Operation Red Wings (US DoD)

He calmly provided his unit's location and the size of the enemy force while requesting immediate support for his team. At one point he was shot in the back causing him to drop the transmitter. Murphy picked it back up, completed the call and continued firing at the enemy that were closing in. Severely wounded, Murphy returned to his cover position with his men and continued the battle.

An MH-47 Chinook helicopter, with eight additional SEALs and eight members of the US Army's 160th Special Operations Aviation Regiment (known as the Night Stalkers) aboard, was sent in as part of an extraction mission to pull out the four embattled SEALs. However, as the Chinook raced to the battle, a rocket-propelled grenade struck the helicopter, killing all 16 men aboard. On the ground and nearly out of ammunition, the four SEALs, Murphy, Luttrell, Dietz and Axelson, continued the fight. By the end of a two-hour gunfight that had careened through the hills and over cliffs, Murphy, Axelson, and Dietz had been killed. An estimated 35 Taliban were also dead. The fourth SEAL, Luttrell, was blasted over a ridge by a rocket propelled grenade and knocked unconscious. Regaining consciousness some time later, he managed to escape – badly injured – and slowly crawled away down the side of a cliff. Dehydrated, with a bullet wound to one leg, shrapnel embedded in both legs, and three vertebrae cracked, the situation was grim.

As the only survivor of the mission, Luttrell descended the mountain but collapsed, unconscious, with a number of fractures and other serious wounds. He regained consciousness and was rescued by a local Pashtun, who ultimately saved Luttrell's life. In his condition, without assistance, he would probably have been killed or captured by the enemy. The Pashtun named Mohammad Gulab Khan from the mountain village of Salar Ban took Luttrell into his home in accordance with the Pashtunwali custom of Nanawatai to give asylum and protection to a person from their enemies. Gulab then invoked the assistance

By the end of the two-hour gunfight that careened through the hills and over cliffs, Murphy, Axelson, and Dietz had been killed. (US DoD)

AFGHANISTAN 23

CHAPTER TWO

An MH-47 Chinook helicopter, with eight additional SEALs and eight US Army 'Night Stalkers' aboard, was sent in as part of an extraction mission to pull out the four embattled SEALs following Operation Red Wings. However, the aircraft was shot down and all onboard perished. (US DoD)

and the Taliban, who were alleged to be just 400 in number. SMA was alleged to have been involved in the opium business and in the eyes of British civil servants he was not the person they wanted in Helmand and the Foreign and Commonwealth Office (FCO) pressed for his removal. Some British officers feared that dismissing SMA would be a repeat of the disastrous decision made in 2003 by the US led Coalition Provisional Authority in Iraq. It had disbanded the Iraqi army which had resulted in thousands of unemployed soldiers joining the insurgency to earn money and feed their families. In Iraq, attacks had soared, and the concern was that the same could happen in Helmand. The US, who had special forces in the area and knew SMA, encouraged the British to retain Akhundzada – mainly because he knew the area, had influence across the community, and had a 3,000 strong militia. But the FCO demanded SMA was dismissed, and he was replaced. Many senior British

of fellow villagers to help protect Luttrell until American forces could be contacted. After word was received of his survival, Luttrell and Gulab were recovered by the USAF Pararescue team from the 59th Expeditionary Rescue Squadron. Based on Luttrell's descriptions of the area, the rescue team returned to the site of the battle two days later and retrieved the remains of Dietz, Murphy, and Axelson. In total 19 US personnel died. It was the worst single-day for US forces since Operation Enduring Freedom had commenced and the single largest loss of life for Naval Special Warfare since World War Two.

Wider Security

NATO now rolled out its plan to broaden security across the country which had been approved by the UN Security Council in 2003. This involved deploying forces to the north in what was called Stage One – eventually Stage Two would encompass the west of the country, Stage Three to the south and Stage Four in the east. Troops from Germany, Sweden, Hungary, and Norway deployed to the north, while Spain, Lithuania, Italy, and the United States moved into the west in 2005. The staged NATO ISAF expansion was building success and had a positive role in extending the authority and influence of the Kabul government to the provinces. The security expansion also helped Afghan regional authorities provide security for the local parliamentary elections in September 2005.

On December 8, 2005, at NATO Headquarters in Brussels, allied foreign ministers endorsed a plan that paved the way for Stage Three, with the United Kingdom agreeing to move into the south of Afghanistan and Canadian troops moving into the east. The British had agreed to move into Helmand province, deep in southern Afghanistan. It was here that members of the Taliban who had fled Kandahar had reformed. A former warlord Sher Mohammed Akhundzada controlled the province. Known locally as SMA, he held the post of provincial governor and with his connection to President Karzai, through marriage, was a powerful and influential man. He dominated the province in 'Afghan style', with an 'iron fist' using a large and powerful 3,000 strong militia to control the community

After word was received of his survival, US Navy Seal Luttrell and Gulab were recovered by the USAF Pararescue team from the 59th Expeditionary Rescue Squadron. (US DoD)

officers acknowledged that SMA was corrupt and accepted the FCO decision. But they failed to appreciate the impact of dismissing the governor and his power in Helmand. Overnight the 400 strong Taliban force, which SMA and his men had pledged to control was given a recruitment boost as SMA's 3,000 armed militiamen joined the insurgents. When he left office SMA told his men to go and join the Taliban in order to get a wage. In an interview with a British newspaper, in 2009, he said: "When I was no longer governor the government stopped paying for the people who supported me. I sent 3,000 of them off to the Taliban because I could not afford to support them, but the Taliban was making payments. Lots of people, including my family members, went back to the Taliban because they had lost respect for the government. The British bore the brunt of this because the Taliban became the defenders of Helmand, where the local tradition doesn't allow foreigners to go into people's ➲

Tony Blair, the then UK Prime Minister agreed to move troops into the south, while Canadian forces would be based in the east. (Canadian Armed Forces)

AFGHANISTAN 25

CHAPTER TWO

The Canadians also deployed Leopard tanks to Kandahar. (ISAF)

Canadian soldiers were deployed at Kandahar airbase and mounted operations across the east of Afghanistan. (Canadian Armed Forces)

homes." The difficult decision regarding SMA was to have far reaching consequences for the British.

The UK government declined to confirm that its forces were preparing to move into Helmand which was now dubbed the most dangerous place on earth and listed by the media as 'Hell-mand'. NATO was now focussed on building the PRT plan across the country and agreed to increase cooperation between the ISAF 'stability mission' and the US-led offensive, Operation Enduring Freedom. By late 2005, it was announced that the United Kingdom-led Allied Rapid Reaction Corps (ARRC) would, from May 2006 until February 2007, lead ISAF forces with Lieutenant General David Richards heading the force. The UK now confirmed that an advance force would deploy to the Helmand desert and build a base for the force which would arrive in 2006.

Hunt for al-Zawahiri

President George Bush had, as part of his war on terror plan, given the Central Intelligence

Agency (CIA) the authority to the hunt down and kill people designated as enemy combatants – otherwise known as 'high value targets'. In early January 2006, the CIA received information about the location of a high value target – Ayman al-Zawahiri. He was an Egyptian born physician, who was wanted by the US for his role in the bombing of the US embassy in Kenya in 1998 and the Bali bombings in 2002. In 2006 he was Osama bin Laden's second in command and the CIA had spent months hunting him down.

They located al-Zawahiri at the village of Damadola in the tribal area of the Pakistan border and on January 13, 2006 a targeted operation was launched in which an unmanned Predator drone armed with four Hellfire missiles hit what was believed to be al-Zawahiri's house. In total 18 people died, but it was later revealed that al-Zawahiri was not among the casualties. The incident sparked protests across Pakistan and fuelled support for both al-Qaeda and the Taliban. On January 26, 2006, just a day before the London Conference on Afghanistan, which created the framework for the next phase of development in the country, the then Secretary of State for Defence, John Reid MP, confirmed the deployment to Helmand of 3,300 British military personnel. He added that the dangers of military action in Afghanistan paled in comparison to the risks Britain would face if the international community allowed the country to become a sanctuary for international terrorism again. Intelligence staff now raised questions about the limited 3,300 UK force against a Taliban which had swelled from 400 to 4,400. The significance of the imbalance was yet to be revealed.

A force of 850 soldiers, mainly drawn from 39 Engineer Regiment RE now deployed in advance to build the base, to be called Camp Bastion. Constructing Camp Bastion, which would provide a secure base from which rotary and fixed wing aircraft could operate, was an extraordinary feat of engineering and logistical operation unparalleled in modern British

Ayman al-Zawahiri. He was an Egyptian born physician, who was wanted by the US for his role in the 1998 bombing of the US embassy in Kenya and the Bali bombings in 2002. (US DoD)

Special forces had located- Ayman al-Zawahiri, bin Laden's right hand man, who was killed in an operation in January 2006. (US DoD)

AFGHANISTAN **27**

CHAPTER TWO

The Taliban attacked an Afghan National Army convoy on Highway 611 in Helmand province - the main route from Kandahar to Ghereshk. In response two RAF Harriers were deployed. (UK MoD)

the Dutch vehicles was hit by an RPG, but it was able to continue. The coalition force then established itself in a defensive position in preparation for further attacks. By the end of the fighting a total of 13 Taliban soldiers had been killed.

In March, Taliban activity in Helmand spiked just weeks before the British were due to arrive. The fighting erupted when insurgents attacked an Afghan National Army convoy on Highway 611, the main route from Kandahar to Ghereshk. In response, two RAF Harriers were deployed along with two US Army Apache

military history. The Sappers and supporting units that built the base, which was in effect a small town, completed it in just four months. Almost everything was flown in by Chinook helicopter and, despite the odds against it, the camp was completed on time. Prior to its subsequent expansion in 2009, Bastion was initially four miles long by two miles wide, incorporating an airfield and tented accommodation for troops. Camp Bastion would later be extended with a second camp, called Camp Leatherneck, which was home to thousands of US Marines. In late April 2006, as the British force prepared move into Helmand, the Taliban, boosted with their new recruits, launched a major offensive to demonstrate their capability at the town of Tarin Kowt,

northeast of Helmand province. A joint US, Australian, and Dutch operation was tasked to protect the town. They came under intense fire and the coalition was forced to withdraw several times. At one point an Australian vehicle suffered a mechanical issue and was unable to leave. It became a target for the insurgents but thankfully the Dutch managed to distract them long enough to allow the Australians to repair their vehicle and pull back.

A month later as the British were moving into Helmand the Dutch-Australian offensive moved north into the Chora Valley. While moving through an open area, devoid of cover, the joint force came under attack by the Taliban, who fired at them with mortars and rockets. Moving back to higher ground, one of

In Colchester, Essex, soldiers were issued with additional equipment and given their final leave as the advance elements of the force flew out to Afghanistan in April. (DPL)

A joint US, Australian, and Dutch operation was tasked to protect the town. They came under intense fire and the coalition force had to withdraw several times. (Netherlands MoD)

The Canadians were constantly in contact with the enemy in firefights in and around Kandahar (Canadian Armed Forces)

attack helicopters. The convoy was heading for Lashkar Gah and was further delayed when vehicles at the head of the column hit a roadside bomb. In darkness, late in the evening, a Quick Reaction Force of 40 soldiers from the 1st Battalion Princess Patricia's Canadian Light Infantry deployed in US helicopters from Kandahar to escort the convoy. Four hours later, the convoy and Canadian escort made it to Lashkar Gah. US forces at the base conducted a defensive patrol, confident that the insurgents had withdrawn but minutes later the Taliban attacked, and Sgt John T Stone was shot in the stomach. The first Canadian to die in combat in the war, Private Robert Costall was laying down covering fire together with Chris Fernandez-Ledon. Costall was shot once through the back of the head, and once in the chest. Master Warrant Officer Ray Brodeur was shot in the leg and the midriff, and two other Canadians were also wounded, as was an American – all from a single American Humvee which fired three to five bursts at friendly positions before being ordered to cease fire when it was realised that he was firing on friendly forces. A US B-52 was called in and dropped bombs on the insurgents, killing more than 40.

Heading for 'Hell-mand'

In Colchester, Essex, soldiers were issued with additional equipment and given their final leave as the advance elements of the force flew out to Afghanistan in April. This would be the first operational deployment for the British Army's new Apache attack helicopter. This new machine would deliver a generational change in fire support to troops in contact and its crews would save hundreds of lives. Prior to deployment, a series of exercises had been conducted on Salisbury Plain, a training area in Wiltshire, during which troops were trained how to direct Apache pilots to lock their machine gun onto specific enemy positions. Scimitar armoured reconnaissance vehicles and Spartan command platform were also being prepared for deployment while politicians sought to 'play down' the role of the British Army as being very much a peace keeping mission.

The deployment plan was to base 3rd Battalion the Parachute Regiment battle group, which included the 1st Battalion the Royal Irish Regiment and the 5th Battalion Royal Regiment of Scotland (Argyll & Sutherland Highlanders), in Camp Bastion with a provincial reconstruction team based at Lashkar Gah, where a small US force had been based. The headquarters of 16 Air Assault Brigade was based in Kandahar where it was co-located with Canadian and US forces. Among the early units to arrive was the Pathfinder Group, the reconnaissance force of 16 Air Assault Brigade whose main task was to act as the 'eyes and ears' of the Task Force, identifying threats and collating intelligence. Everything was focused on delivering development to the Afghans in the form of basic infrastructure. To those who have no vision of Helmand, imagine a scorched desert, dotted with small communities. Very few families have electricity or running water in their homes and the majority sleep on the floor in properties that people in the west would describe as 'sub standard' – and that is being gracious. Very few had cars or pickups, and the most common form of transport was a motorbike. Employment was seasonal, with farming as the main source of income and the poppy harvest the pinnacle of the growing season. For the soldiers who arrived in Helmand it was like stepping back in time, but the one commodity that many appeared to have despite the intermittent power supply was a mobile phone. This as time went on would become a powerful tool in the insurgents' intimidation of local communities and their ability to direct and plan attacks.

In London, the planning and expectation of the deployment had been based around the force providing security and stability in order to allow the delivery of reconstruction. However, as Brigadier Ed Butler, the commander of 16 Air Assault Brigade, and his headquarters commenced their pre-deployment training on Exercise Herrick Eagle, there was little information to draw on and no strategic plan. The media had dubbed the region 'Hell-mand' and the 'Desert of Death' – temperatures soared during the day and plummeted at night. Those arriving had been prepared for conflict but briefed that their task would in the main be a peace support role – providing security while reconstruction took place. As soldiers landed in Kandahar they went into temporary accommodation and underwent a refresher package of acclimatisation and combat readiness called RSOI (Reception, Staging and Onward Integration).

At one point an Australian vehicle suffered a mechanical issue and was unable to leave. It became a target for the insurgents. The Dutch managed to distract the insurgents long enough to allow the Australians to repair their vehicle and pull back. (Australian DoD)

CHAPTER THREE

BAPTISM OF FIRE

In 2006, coalition ISAF's main focus was on Helmand in southern Afghanistan. Here British troops were to deploy in the spring as part of NATO's (ISAF) stage three delivery of security and reconstruction. The largest and most volatile province in the country, it had been described as the most dangerous place on earth and the Americans who had a small force in the area warned the UK that the Taliban would come out fighting.

Since the Taliban had been ousted from power in Kabul they had reformed in Helmand and re-established old smuggling routes for weapons and explosives. British paratroopers were ready for anything after months of training and briefings. It was public knowledge that the governor had been sacked and his militia had signed up with the Taliban but staggeringly, politicians and political advisors had decided that there was no hard evidence that the 3,000-strong armed militia had switched allegiance. But they were waiting, and after a couple of months watching the soldiers, the paras faced some of the most brutal face-to face fighting since the Korean War.

The main role of the UK force had intended to be to set the security conditions to allow development take place. The Ministry of Defence, alongside the Department for International Development (DFID) and the Foreign and Commonwealth Office (FCO), developed what was called the Helmand Plan, with the FCO taking the lead on policy. The plan sought to secure what was called an 'ink spot' of security in Helmand, around the provincial capital of Lashkar Gar and the busy town of Gereshk, forming a 'triangle of security' in which a stable environment would allow

British soldiers soon found themselves facing daily attacks as the Taliban attempted to stop their move into Helmand. (DPL)

development to grow. The aim was to establish security in one area and then expand it across Helmand. There was good reasoning behind the plan: Lashkar Gah was the agricultural 'breadbasket' of the region where farmers sold their produce in the markets, while Gereshk, with its 'gateway road' to Kandahar, was strategically important for trade. Situated within the Nahr Saraj district and enjoying a strong local economy, Gereshk sat on a key road known as Highway One, built during the Soviet occupation and connecting Helmand to the regional city of Kandahar, just 78 miles away. It was a vital road for business. It was also known as the 'Highway to Hell', coalition forces and convoys were regularly attacked while the Taliban attempted to establish its own vehicle check points. The area between Lashkar Gah and Gereshk was defined as the Afghan Development Zone (ADZ) in which DFID and the FCO would, after security was achieved, direct projects to improve local living conditions and governance.

Improvised Explosive Devices (IEDs) were being used by insurgents in Iraq and with the help of Iranian instruction the Taliban started to use them. (US DoD)

Ready for Anything

The UK force strength was set at 3,300 and while on paper the manpower looked sufficient, in reality only a third of this number represented the infantry battle group on the ground, that was around 1,000 troops. The remainder being assigned to logistics, force protection, and headquarter duties. Of the infantry force 150 were assigned to duties at Laskhar Gah and 200 directed to training and mentoring the Afghan National Army – the remaining 650 paratroopers would be responsible for security.

They were 'ready for anything' and had spent almost a year training, but it quickly became apparent that theirs was a huge challenge. Helmand was a significant area to secure, a total 20,000 square miles, the same size as Wales, but while more than 9,000 police officers deliver security across the Welsh nation, British

Lashkar Gah, the market town, and regional capital where the British based their headquarters in southern Afghanistan. (DPL)

Helicopters provided commanders with the element of speed and surprise and avoided the risk of roadside bombs. (DPL)

CHAPTER THREE

The British area stretched from Musa Qaleh in the north to Garmsir in the south of Helmand province. (UK MoD)

British paratroopers regroup after a firefight with insurgents in Nowzad, just weeks after arriving in Helmand. (DPL)

Chinook helicopters land to extract British troops after an operation at a village near Nowzad. (UK MoD)

commanders had a fraction of that number to manage a lawless province run by the Taliban, armed drug lords, and criminals engaged in a struggle for power. The British had the support of Danish and Estonian forces as well as Afghan security forces, but the Afghans were poorly trained, unreliable, and corrupt. And a large number were 'in the pocket' of the Taliban.

In his book *Danger Close*, Lieutenant Colonel Stuart Tootal, the commanding officer of 3 PARA in 2006, wrote: "Even if our operations could be limited to the region around Lashkar Gar and Gereshk as we planned, it was still a huge area for the limited number of troops that I would have at my disposal." The first few weeks seemed quiet; the paras were attacked in earlier May when several shots were fired at a patrol. The incident was dismissed as 'insignificant', but the platoon commander was convinced the paras were being tested. In Gereshk, a relatively prosperous area compared to other parts of Helmand, soldiers continued to find local children to be welcoming. The shallow smiles of shopkeepers, however, told a different story, the concern in their faces highlighting an anxiety of not wanting to be seen as 'friendly'. These human indicators sent a clear signal that the Taliban were around. Indeed, they may well have been standing among the locals, just watching how they reacted to the troops. The tempo of operations now increased.

On May 19, a convoy of Afghan, American, and French soldiers was attacked on the main

32   www.keymilitary.com

road between Sangin and Kajaki. Reports indicated as many as 15 Afghans had been killed and others missing. Paratroopers boarded two Chinooks, escorted by AH-64 Apache helicopters. In the darkness, however, it was hard to locate the missing men, and a second search resumed at first light when locals handed over the bodies of the two missing French soldiers and nine Afghans. The vehicles later limped into a forward operating base Robinson.

Platoon House Strategy

Attacks now spiked and at Musa Qaleh insurgents attempted to overrun the town's district centre (DC) – the equivalent of a council or local authority building. These DCs were official government buildings and thus held in high regard by politicians in Kabul - although to the naked eye they appeared to be nothing more than crumbling ⮕

The British Army's Apache helicopter made its debut in Helmand in 2006, pilots were often called on to provide supressing fire from the machine gun mounted under the aircraft. (DPL)

CHAPTER THREE

US Air Force A-10 Thunderbolts – often called the Warthog – was regularly called for to provide close air support to troops engaged in firefights with the enemy. (DPL)

A mobile phone picture captures the aftermath of a firefight after paratroopers counterattacked the Taliban following an ambush. (DPL)

buildings within a compound. For President Karzai they were a symbol of the government's authority, and he did not want them overrun by insurgents. The British had deployed troops to support the Afghan government and Governor Daoud had the impression that they were under his direct command. He pressed Colonel Charlie Knaggs, who headed the regional Provisional Reconstruction Team in Helmand and Brigadier Ed Butler, the Commander of the British force to deploy troops to protect the DCs in Sangin, Musa Qaeda, and Nowzad, but Brig Butler resisted his demands. Putting troops into permanent outposts was not part of the British plan. Indeed, Butler suggested it would play straight into the Taliban's hands and allow them to attack the buildings. The British troops would in effect become 'sitting ducks' for the insurgents. However, Daoud continued to place pressure on Butler. The UK government now faced a difficult decision in responding to the Daoud's anxieties. Karzai had direct access to Lieutenant General Sir David Richards, then serving as the commander of ISAF, and expressed his concerns. Whatever he personally felt to be the best course of action, Butler was forced to deploy troops across Helmand in what became known as the 'platoon house' strategy. It was a strategy that was to become highly controversial, some would say disastrous, and ultimately left the Gereshk plan for security in ruins. In late May, the security situation continued to worsen and troops from 3 PARA and supporting arms were deployed to secure the DCs at Now Zad, Gereshk, Sangin, and Musa Qaleh. Troops were also deployed to Kajaki to protect the dam and by the end of the month planning was underway for a search and cordon operation at Now Zad where intelligence had indicated that the Taliban were forming up in numbers. On June 4, A Company 3 PARA was tasked with mounting a cordon and search of a walled compound to the east of Now Zad which quickly turned into a major fire-fight. The mission, codenamed Operation Mutay, was part of a larger US plan and the paras faced machine gun fire from multiple directions. After several hours of extensive fighting, they called in close air support and were supported by both Apache helicopters and USAF A-10 Warthogs to suppress the insurgents. After the operation, a paratrooper in A Company told BBC reporter Paul Wood that it was unnerving to see the enemy running towards you with such determination. He said: "You just had to keep cool and make sure every shot counted; the more they came, the more we dropped. It was intense and nothing prepares you for it, you simply go into training mode and deliver everything you have been trained to do".

Face-to-Face fighting

Brig Butler's warnings were now becoming a reality – Sangin, Musa Qaleh, and Now Zad were now under constant attack and soldiers were dying. The enemy appeared to be 'cocaine loaded' and in firefights would, despite being

The district centre in Musa Qaleh. These official buildings were in poor condition and very old but regarded by the government in Kabul as very important. (DPL)

Paratroopers wore helmets, but their body armour provided limited protection and was about to be upgraded. (UK MoD)

position, forcing them to withdraw. With nothing further to be gained, Lt Farmer took the decision to withdraw back towards the DC. However, during the opening exchange the platoon's two prisoners had been killed by enemy fire, a fact of which the Taliban were obviously unaware. As further insurgents appeared on the scene, the Taliban began a determined pursuit of 1 Platoon, clearly intent on recovering the two prisoners. One Platoon was then engaged by a second group of enemy on the other side of the canal that runs north to south across the area.

The paras succeeded in suppressing this enemy position with heavy fire and the platoon began to move towards the wadi. The two HCR armoured vehicles in the wadi had been manoeuvring into positions to provide fire support but they had not been able to

shot, continue to run at British troops, like zombies. In Sangin, the Taliban had increased their use of stand-off weapons against the DC, firing rockets and mortars against A Company. On August 17, 1 Platoon, commanded by Lieutenant Hugo Farmer, was on patrol south of the HLS, supported by a Scimitar and Spartan from D Squadron HCR. The two armoured vehicles were in the open area of the wadi, while 1 Platoon was in the close country south of the HLS surrounded by corn and maize, narrow tracks, and irrigation ditches. Two individuals, who had clearly been reporting on the patrol's movements, were in the process of being detained but at that moment members of the platoon spotted seven armed Taliban moving nearby. The insurgents observed the platoon at the same time and opened fire. One Platoon mounted a full-blown platoon attack and called in mortar fire on to the Taliban

British troops with their bayonets fixed wait for the order to advance during a cordon and search operation in Sangin. (UK MoD)

The aftermath of a bomb being dropped by close air support near the town of Musa Qaleh. (DPL)

AFGHANISTAN 35

CHAPTER THREE

Local farmers appeared friendly, but many were in the pay of the Taliban and passed information to them about British patrols. (DPL)

The crew of a Scimitar reconnaissance vehicle return fire with their 30mm Rarden cannon during an attack by the Taliban on Sangin. (DPL)

series of compounds. A Land Rover WMIK was with the forward left section while a second, supported by a fire team, was deployed into the town covering approaches to the platoon's right flank. Corporal Bryan Budd was leading the forward right section and, as he advanced, observed three enemy positions to his front, which he indicated to his men while organising them for an attack. As he led them forward the WMIK on his left flank was ambushed, and there was an immediate requirement to regain the initiative. Budd pushed on with the attack that developed into a significant fire fight. One member of his section was hit in his body armour while Lance Corporal Paul Roberts, the MFC (Mortar Fire Controller) attached to the platoon, was hit in the shoulder. As Privates Stephen Halton and Andrew Lanaghan moved to pull Roberts into cover, Lanaghan was hit in the face and arm. Private Halton continued to extract Roberts and Lanaghan while Budd pressed home the attack himself, being wounded in the process. The section second-in-command pulled the section back to regroup, unaware that Corporal Budd had been wounded as he moved forward. His body was later found surrounded by dead Taliban fighters. For his outstanding courage he was awarded the Victoria Cross. Days later in a tragic accident at Kajaki paratroopers walked into a legacy minefield. Cpl Mark Wright organised and directed the rescue despite serious wounds – he was awarded the George Cross.

The situation in Musa Qala was desperate. Much of the town centre had been destroyed in the fighting, and many residents had fled to nearby villages. The market rarely opened, and the entire area had become a ghost town. On August 26, a woman and her child were killed in the bazaar during a firefight. The elders blamed the Taliban and Governor Daoud contacted the Task Force after being told the enemy was ready to talk. The Taliban had suffered heavily in their unsuccessful attempts to capture the DC, but Brig Butler was not prepared to agree to a ceasefire. He was, however, prepared to find a solution that ensured the safety of his men while

engage the insurgents due to the difficulties of target identification through the thick vegetation. As they moved, one of the vehicles, the Spartan, lost a track and was immobilised; at the same time, it attracted attention from the insurgents who soon realised that it was unable to move. With 1 Platoon now visible, the remainder of A Company's fire support weapons were brought to bear, including artillery. This in turn resulted in the Taliban engaging the DC with RPGs from within the town. In the wadi, meanwhile, the HCR recovered the crew and specialist equipment from the Spartan, while A Company moved into positions to prevent the enemy from reaching it. Shortly afterwards, close air support was called in and dropped a bomb which, combined with heavy artillery and mortar fire forced the enemy to abandon the fight for the time being. On August 20, a patrol from 1 Platoon was moving north with two sections deployed forward to provide protection for the third section that was using bar mines to create a covered route through a

Corporal Bryan Budd who received a posthumous Victoria Cross after his courageous action at Sangin in 2006. (UK MoD)

Corporal Mark Wright who saved the lives of his soldiers in a Kajaki minefield was awarded the George Cross. (UK MOD)

the DC, while the elders agreed to support the police and facilitate reconstruction and development projects.

The Battle of Musa Qaleh

At Musa Qaleh on September 1, a mortar attack killed a member of 1 R IRISH, Ranger Anare Draiva, and mortally wounded Corporal Paul Muirhead. A day later, on September 2, an RAF Nimrod MR2 plane on a surveillance mission crashed just outside Kandahar killing all 14 personnel on board. The aircraft, Nimrod XV230, was on a routine reconnaissance mission over Helmand province in Afghanistan, searching for insurgents. It crashed shortly after a catastrophic fire broke out on board, following being refuelled in mid-air. The MR2 was a valuable strategic asset that provided tactical capability. During major operations, using

maintaining security in Musa Qaleh. Major Adam Jowett, the commander of British troops in Musa Qaleh, was convinced that the Taliban were serious, and he arranged a shura, which took place in the desert west of the town. The British were represented by Brig Butler, who was well aware of the need to maintain political and military credibility. He was willing to consider a 'cessation of fighting' in which British forces would maintain their presence in the desert in what was termed an overwatch of the town. This would involve a mobile operations group of Scimitars and light vehicles being based in the desert within striking distance of the town. In the event that the Taliban mounted any act of aggression, the agreement would end immediately. A fourteen-point plan drawn up by Governor Daoud for handing over Musa Qaleh to the elders was gradually implemented. According to this, the flag of Afghanistan would continue to fly over

Paratroopers at Nowzad, distinctive with the netting over their helmets, leave the base for a routine patrol. (UK MoD)

Paratroopers with bayonets fixed clear a compound during an operation. (UK MoD)

AFGHANISTAN

CHAPTER THREE

The Pathfinders in their heavily armed Land Rovers at Musa Qaleh, a town in the north of Helmand which saw significant fighting. (DPL)

the call sign 'Magic', it was able to provide significant intelligence about the Taliban and their movements. The loss of the 14 RAF crew and army personnel aboard the aircraft sent a shock wave through the brigade headquarters in Kandahar and throughout the battle group. On that same day, six more British troops were injured at Musa Qaleh and three days later, the Taliban once again tried to storm the base, but were beaten off by the defenders assisted by RAF Harriers and USAF A-10 Warthogs.

On September 6, a Chinook flew into Musa Qala to evacuate two wounded soldiers who had suffered shrapnel wounds in an attack, but the Taliban were expecting its arrival and ambushed the aircraft, forcing it to turn back. On returning to Camp Bastion, the crew found that the helicopter had been hit four times. Another casualty evacuation mission was flown into Musa Qala later the same day, but this time it was escorted by Apaches, A-10s, and an AC-130 Spectre gunship that suppressed any Taliban fire, enabling the Chinook to complete its mission.

On October 13, Major Adam Jowett's Easy Company was extracted from Musa Qaleh after occupying the base for ten weeks. 3 Commando Brigade RM had started to arrive in late September to relieve 16 Air Assault Brigade and it was elements of 42 Commando RM who

The day of departure from Musa Qaleh after the commander had secured a 'cessation of violence'. (UK MoD)

deployed into the desert to meet Easy Company, who left the town aboard a fleet of Afghan lorries. The elders had promised to guarantee safe passage and an elder climbed on to each lorry. The operation went smoothly without a shot being fired, and the convoy was able to rendezvous safely. The commandos had gradually been arriving since the middle of September at Kandahar, where they underwent a package of briefings and tactical updates. They then flew to Camp Bastion and prepared to deploy by helicopter into the field. In the past the fierce but healthy rivalry between the commandos and paras had always resulted in a frosty tension between the two. However, on this occasion all such rivalry was forgotten. Young paratroopers readily passed on advice and guidance to the commandos while also handing over all available spare items of equipment to them.

A soldier with Easy Company manning a machine gun at Musa Qaleh where the paras and Royal Irish fought a bloody battle. (UK MoD)

Operation Medusa

In July, Canadian and Afghan forces had left the Panjwayi region and once again the Taliban surged back. The beginning of September 2006 saw the start of much more intense fighting in the region again, forcing the Canadians to launch Operation Medusa. On the first day Canadian forces strategically surrounded the Taliban and called in heavy artillery and air strikes while taking no casualties themselves. On the second day, company-sized elements of the Canadian forces moved in to directly challenge the Taliban. Four soldiers were killed in two attacks. Three were killed while assaulting a Taliban position and one was killed in a bomb attack. A day later saw another deadly day, a Canadian soldier was killed, and more than 30 others were wounded when an American A-10 accidentally strafed Canadian troops who had called in air support. For the next few weeks there was heavy fighting on a daily basis and the Taliban who had begun fighting the battle in a conventional way of trenches started to retreat from the battlefield. Canadian forces then faced sporadic resistance until they gained the upper hand. Reconstruction efforts began immediately, and small cells of Taliban fighters returned to their deadly tactics of suicide and roadside bombings.

The reconstruction efforts following Operation Medusa were intended to help the local economy grow but one project in particular was particularly dangerous. Canadian Forces began the construction of a road, code-named 'Summit', from the Panjwayi area to outlying areas including Kandahar city. The purpose of the road was to improve security in the region by providing a paved route into otherwise difficult and close terrain. However, roadside bombs, booby traps, and ambushes targeting engineers who were building the road cost the lives of six Canadians. The road was seen by local farmers as causing problems with the irrigation systems. On October 3, two Canadian soldiers were killed when the Taliban ambushed an observation post which had been set up in the area and on November 21, two Canadian soldiers were injured, one very seriously, when anti-personnel mine was triggered.

Soldiers serving with the Royal Irish Regiment prepare an 81mm mortar at the Musa Qaleh base. (UK MoD)

The Taliban constantly tried to shoot down a Chinook, forcing the pilots to fly low and fast to avoid giving the insurgents time to take aim. (UK MoD)

The Apace was considered a 'game changer' by soldiers as on so many occasions it arrived, and the crew were able to suppress the enemy with their chain gun and Hellfire missiles. (UK MoD)

CHAPTER FOUR

FIGHTING EXPLODES

In 2007, insurgents stepped up their offensive across Afghanistan from Gardez in the east to Kunduz in the north, as well as Uruzgan and Helmand further south. The improvised explosive device (IED) was now the Taliban's weapon of choice, and they quickly learned how to produce them using the most basic of materials.

Explosives were packed around nails and bolts, and sometimes smeared with animal faeces to cause additional medical trauma through infection. They watched troops' patrol patterns and planted devices on pathways, tracks, roads, and compound walls. As time went on, they dug larger roadside bombs deep into the ground and wrapped the explosives in plastic to avoid detection, wiring them up to pressure plates or initiating them by remote control. IEDs were often linked to others in a 'daisy chain' trap, designed to catch troops in a secondary blast.

The impact of the roadside bomb was a 'game changer', and for a short period gave the insurgents the initiative. The fact remained, however, that the Taliban had changed the dynamic of the fighting and for the first time

The fighting in Helmand exploded at the start of 2007 as the insurgents adopted the roadside bomb to enhance their attacks. (UK MoD)

they were 'shaping the battle space'. UK military commanders called for more helicopters which could deliver the elements of speed and surprise and avoid the roadside bombs. But there was political caution, the fear was that if a Chinook were lost with 44 lives it would impact on public support for the war. Instead, UK politicians opted to embark on a programme of purchasing a new generation of vehicles designed to provide greater protection from mines and roadside bombs – many of which were also being deployed to Iraq. These included the Mastiff 6x6 armoured patrol vehicle and the Ridgeback 4x4 Mine-Resistant Ambush Protected (MRAP) vehicle, both of which provided soldiers with greater protection against roadside bombs, mines, and ambushes. Also, in the inventory of new vehicles to be deployed in Afghanistan was the Jackal 4x4 Light Patrol Vehicle but, as in most cases, there was a compromise which impacted on operations.

The heavily armoured Mastiff, although offering a high level of protection, lacked speed and manoeuvrability, while the highly mobile Jackal performed excellently on roads and tracks, but in the desert sand its wheels

The Taliban's Improvised Explosive Devices (IEDs) increased in size forcing politicians to purchase a new generation of vehicles designed to provide greater protection from mines and roadside bombs. (DPL)

Helicopter capability was now more important than ever, but there was political caution, the fear was that if a Chinook was lost with 44 lives it would impact on public support for the war. (UK MoD)

frequently sank due to the weight of the vehicle. A further limitation of all soft-skinned and armoured vehicles, whatever their design and configuration, is that they unavoidably generate clouds of sand or dust as they move at any speed in dry or desert conditions. In Afghanistan these sent clear signals to the Taliban and thus the element of surprise was frequently lost.

Taking the fight to the enemy
US General Dan McNeill, who commanded coalition forces, wanted to hit the insurgents hard and take the fight to the enemy in a series of operations across the spring and summer months. In March 2007, NATO launched Operation Achilles with the aim of clearing the Taliban from Helmand, where the British were based. US paratroopers from the 82nd Airborne moved into the Ghorak Valley to the east of Sangin, while Danish, Canadian, Dutch, Polish, and Afghan units joined the mission with the UK's 45 Commando clearing 25 enemy compounds around the Kajaki area. By the end of April, ISAF troops, including Afghan National Army ground forces, pushed north through the Sangin Valley driving the

CHAPTER FOUR

The Canadians were based in Kandahar and deployed their LAV armoured wheeled vehicles at the battle of Medusa. (Canadian MoD)

The Dutch deployed their heavily armoured Bushmaster vehicles which provided protection against roadside bombs. (DPL)

Taliban from Gereshk and the surrounding villages. It was reported that coalition troops, backed by air support, killed more than 130 Taliban fighters. At the same time US and coalition troops mounted offensive operations in Herat to prevent the Taliban swarming back into Helmand. As coalition forces went on the offensive the Taliban's most senior commander was snared in May 2007. Mullah Dadullah Ajkhund, known as 'the butcher', was located in Helmand and killed in an operation by ISAF special forces. This was a major intelligence success for the coalition. But as the summer fighting season continued insurgents continued their onslaught.

At the town of Chora in Uruzgan province which bordered Kandahar and Helmand more than 200 fighters attempted to take control of the entire district. In mid-June Dutch troops who were working on reconstruction projects to build a school and repair a mosque came under fire. A Dutch convoy was attacked by a suicide bomber killing a soldier and on June 16, a US Air Force A-10 spotted a large group of insurgents moving towards the town. A short while later three Afghan police posts

After the Taliban captured the police post at Sarab, the Dutch responded with heavy artillery fire and called in Apache helicopters. (DPL)

at Kala Kala, Nyazi, and Sarab on the main road linking Chora to Tarinkot came under coordinated attack by a group of more than 800 fighters. The Taliban captured the Sarab police post - executing policemen and their families. The Dutch responded with heavy artillery fire and called in Apache helicopters. Additional Dutch and Australian troops based at Camp Holland in Tarinkot moved to Chora to mount a counterattack. Over Sunday and Monday, June 17/18, more Dutch reinforcements arrived from Camp Holland increasing the number of Dutch troops at Chora to 500. In a firefight that lasted all day the Dutch regained control, having called in F-16s to support their operation. The fighting, at a time when the Taliban had changed their method of warfare and adopted the IED, it was the largest insurgent direct offensive of 2007. As a result of the fighting one American, two Dutch, and 16 Afghan soldiers and 91 Taliban fighters died.

Hostage crisis

On July 19, 2007, a group of 23 South Korean missionaries were captured and taken for hostage by members of the Taliban while passing through Ghazni province. The coalition feared this could be a major incident with the insurgents executing the hostages to gain maximum publicity. US special forces monitored the situation, but the South Korean government sought a negotiated release.

The group, composed of 16 women and seven men, was captured while travelling from Kandahar to Kabul by bus on a mission sponsored by the Saemmul Presbyterian Church. The crisis began when two local men, who the driver had allowed to board, started shooting to bring the bus to a halt. Over the next month, the hostages were kept in cellars and farmhouses and regularly moved in groups of three to four. In late July, two of the hostages, Bae Hyeong-gyu, a 42-year-old South Korean pastor of the Saemmul Church, and Shim Seong-min, a 29-year-old South Korean

The US Marines pause during an operation, minutes after a fighter aircraft had dropped bombs on a Taliban position. (DPL)

CHAPTER FOUR

Dutch Bushmaster vehicles in Afghanistan. The Netherlands deployed 1,900 troops in Afghanistan and was the first NATO country to end its combat mission in the country. (DPL)

man, were killed. Later, with negotiations making progress, two women, Kim Gyeong-ja and Kim Ji-na, were released on August 19 and the remaining 19 hostages handed over at the end of the month. The release of the hostages was secured with a South Korean promise to withdraw its 200 troops from Afghanistan by the end of 2007. They had been based in Kabul and although the South Korean government offered no statement, a Taliban spokesman claimed that they had been paid a ransom of US$ 20m in exchange for the safety of the captured missionaries.

Apache Rescue

In Helmand, the UK Commando Brigade moved to maintain pressure on the Taliban by forcing them to go on the defensive and disrupting their activities in Garmsir. In January, the brigade launched an operation to demonstrate that the coalition was capable of operating anywhere it chose. It also wanted to psychologically disorientate the Taliban and leave them on the back foot. The key objective was Jugroom Fort southwest of Garmsir where a large number of enemy forces were known to be based, among them local commanders. It sat on a feature overlooking an expanse of desert, had high walls and would be difficult to attack. To reach it, the marines would have to cross a river, then drive across open ground towards the objective in their Viking Armoured Personnel vehicles that offered little protection from enemy fire.

Prior to the assault a five-hour bombardment of artillery, mortars, B-1 bombers, F/A-18 Hornets, and AH-64 Apache attack helicopters would hit the fort hard and eliminate the enemy

Australian forces moved to the area to support the Dutch counter-attack at Chora. (Australian MoD)

Coalition forces were now mounting more operations to push the Taliban out of the country. (UK MoD)

before Zulu Company dismounted and entered the complex. The force had access to the Nimrod MR-2s' live imaging feed and planned for Zulu Company to strike just before dawn, kill any remaining insurgents, and destroy their equipment. When satisfied that they had accomplished their mission, the marines would withdraw back over the river and regroup at their assembly area. A lack of resources meant this would once again be a raid as the brigade did not have sufficient troops to capture and hold ground. In essence, the plan was to 'assault the fort in a deliberate attack in order to disrupt and harass the Taliban on their own ground, to raid and not occupy, to get in fast and get out fast'. However, only three troops of Zulu Company were available as the other two were committed elsewhere. While The Light Dragoons and armoured support group in their tracked vehicles pushed the number of troops on the ground close to 200, the actual 'bayonet strength' of Zulu Company would be limited to less than 100. Having moved from the assembly area to their forming up point (FUP), the marines boarded their Vikings and awaited the word to launch the operation. As they did so, a diversionary attack on other two positions, designated Objectives 'Helvellyn' and 'Snowdon', was launched by India Company to create confusion. Then, at about 0200 hrs, B-1 bombers attacked the fort. Their task was to destroy the fortifications and breach the wall in the southwest corner through which the assaulting marines could mount an assault. In total, 20 2,000lb bombs were dropped to breach the wall and provide an entry point for Zulu Company.

As first light approached the marines were ready to advance across the river to the objective, but the move from the 'start line' was delayed until 0630 hrs. Finally, they received the order to board their vehicles, three Vikings for each troop and two for Company TAC HQ with 5 Troop taking the lead and 1 and 4 Troops following. As they crossed the fast-flowing river, section commanders gave the order to fix bayonets. Space on the far side of the river was limited. 5 Troop, TAC HQ and 1 Troop crossed while 4 Troop's Vikings crossed the first part of the river and stopped on a spit of land south of the second part of the crossing. As the Vikings halted in a line, the marines dismounted. The ground was soft and riddled with irrigation ditches that made progress difficult, but 5 Troop advanced rapidly to the breach in the wall and took cover to the left of it. As they did so, they came under a hail of gunfire, RPGs, and mortar bombs. A marine threw a grenade through the breach entry point in the wall and, immediately after it exploded, members of 5 Troop assaulted into the fort. Several injuries were quickly reported over the company radio communications net as the Taliban continued to throw grenades and launch RPGs at the assaulting marines. An RPG bounced off the helmet of Marine Matty Corcoran, while Lieutenant Matt Hammond, the commander of 5 Troop, had

Dutch, British, US, Italian, and Canadian fighter aircraft were based at Kandahar and Bagram from where they supported operations on the ground. (US DoD)

AFGHANISTAN 45

CHAPTER FOUR

Viking and later Warthog armoured vehicles were used by the armoured support group to ferry soldiers across Helmand. (UK MoD)

The commandos mounted the assault on Jugroom Fort to disrupt the Taliban in the region. (UK MoD)

In January the UK Commando Brigade launched an operation to demonstrate that the coalition was capable of operating anywhere it chose. It also wanted to psychologically disorientate the Taliban and leave them on the defensive. (UK MoD)

During the battle at Jugroom Fort one of the Apache pilots suggested that the helicopters could lift four marines, two strapped to the outside of each aircraft and recover the missing commando. (US DoD)

A picture from the second Apache showing the rescue team on the side of the Apaches. (UK MoD)

a lucky escape when a 7.62mm bullet from an AK-47 hit a knife he was carrying on his belt and ricocheted off. Such was the level of sustained firepower brought to bear by the attacking force that one of its fire-support teams (FST) fired 2,000 rounds and for more than 45 minutes the Joint Terminal Attack Controller (JTAC) - the person who directs the fighter aircraft and helicopters - deployed with Zulu Company was directing Apache fire missions against identified insurgents. Having eliminated all the enemy they could see, the marines prepared to withdraw. The wounded having been loaded into a Viking, the force broke contact with the enemy and withdrew across the river. As they did so, 105mm artillery fire and Apache helicopters, with 30mm cannon and Hellfire missiles, began again to bring fire to bear on the fort to cover the withdrawal. At this juncture, a report was heard over the radio net that a marine was missing. It was quickly established that LCpl Matthew Ford, of 5 Troop, was absent and was still in the fort. All feared the worst that LCpl Ford had been taken prisoner, but no-one said a word.

It was now daylight and just before 0800 hrs. The Taliban could observe the raiding force's position and thus to race back across the river would be potential suicide. Nevertheless, the marines of Zulu Company had no reservations about going back to rescue

The US 82nd Airborne spearhead the coalition assault to retake Musa Qaleh. (DPL)

a missing comrade. Time was running out and as the Apaches circled overhead, one of the pilots made a bold proposal. He called up the raiding force and suggested that two Apaches could lift four marines, two strapped to the outside of each aircraft, to the fort to retrieve the missing man and then fly them all out, the entire operation taking only a few minutes. Protection would be provided by two more Apaches loitering overhead. The plan was agreed and flying in at low level at just 50kts, one Apache landed south of the wall as planned but unfortunately, due to the smoke and dust on the objective, the other aircraft landed on the north side. The two men who landed south of the wall swiftly located LCpl Ford lying close to the wall. Sadly, he had sustained fatal injuries. The following day Zulu Company held a memorial service for their fallen comrade.

US troops assaulted Musah Qaleh by Chinook helicopters while the larger percentage of the force arrived by vehicle. (DPL)

Coalition air power had mounted numerous fire missions to suppress the enemy before the assault on Jugroom Fort commenced. (DPL)

CHAPTER FOUR

British and Afghan National Army forces drive towards Musa Qaleh. (UK MoD)

IEDs were a major threat at Musa Qaleh where the enemy had seeded roadside bombs in the approaches to the town. (DPL)

Battle to Retake Musa Qaleh

Since late 2006, Musa Qaleh had been back in the hands of the insurgents who used the town as a base from which to launch attacks into the Sangin Valley, flying their flag in defiance of the Afghan government. ISAF wanted the Taliban removed and US and ISAF troops would be assigned to the British operation.

Behind the scenes a key Taliban commander, Mullah Abdul Salaam Alizai, had been talking direct to President Kaizai's officials about switching sides. The Alizai was the dominant tribe in the town, and he was the leader of one of the three sub-tribes. The secret talks went on for months and there was clearly a split within the Taliban in Musa Qaleh and commanders sought to exploit this weakness. Planning was now underway to capture the town and Mullah Salaam indicated his men could lead an uprising against the Taliban in the town. The mission, led by the British 52 Brigade was codenamed Operation Mar Kardad and involved significant support from US forces as well as others from Denmark, Estonia, and the Afghan National Army. It was officially announced as being 'Afghan planned, and Afghan led'.

Preliminary operations had begun in November when 40 Commando RM, deployed in Vikings, moved north across the Helmand River, while the Scots Guards and King's Royal Hussars in their Warriors and Mastiffs moved to an area east of Musa Qaleh. In the middle of that month, the Ministry of Defence reported that troops from 40 Cdo RM and Right Flank (company) of the Scots Guards were patrolling outside the town to confuse the Taliban insurgents and disrupt their supply routes. Meanwhile, 52 Infantry Brigade's plan, based around an 'influence' approach, had been presented to the head of ISAF and approved in mid-November 2007. His endorsement thus ensured that the operation would be allotted the necessary resources. As the initial 'interdiction' operation began, the enemy made a move on Sangin, launching repeated rocket attacks on the town and also attacking Kajaki,

Commandos used light mortars in their operation to help retake the town of Musa Qaleh. (UK MoD)

The Afghan national flag flies over Musa Qaleh after the coalition successfully ejected the Taliban from the town. (UK MoD)

Now Zad, and Gereshk in a clear move to draw ISAF forces away from the advance on Musa Qaleh.

The mission to recapture Musa Qaleh was focused on an innovative 'Information Operation', to inform the town's 20,000 residents that ISAF forces were going to 'liberate the community from the Taliban', while persuading the insurgents to leave the town. The 'persuasion' would come in the form of an increased ISAF presence around Musa Qaleh. The Taliban leader, Mullah Salaam, was still making promises that he could influence the enemy, but nothing had been agreed and British intelligence suggested he had little control over the main force, which was estimated to number 1,000 -2,000 insurgents. The operation to take Musa Qala was the largest military assault that British forces had undertaken in Afghanistan at the time. As ISAF made its intentions clear, hundreds of people fled the town to avoid any fighting. On December 6, British, Afghan, and US forces started their assault. Initially, the British and Afghan forces attacked in the afternoon, advancing in three separate columns from the south, west, and east of the town and supported by several hundred vehicles.

Close air support, attack helicopters and fighter aircraft, was provided from ISAF based in Kabul. This daylight approach, however, was a feint designed to distract attention from a helicopter-borne landing by a battalion of the US 82nd Airborne Division's 506th Parachute Infantry Regiment. Other elements of the division would be flown in by more than a dozen Chinooks and supporting Black Hawks, protected by Apache attack helicopter escorts, and air assault to an area north of the town. The troops of the 506th, codenamed Task Force Fury, flew direct from Kandahar Airfield and on landing encountered Taliban forces entrenched in fully prepared positions. Meanwhile, the British and Afghans discovered their approach had been seeded with IEDs. Fighting continued through the night with the Americans clearing mines and fortifications as they advanced. On December 7, the first full day of fighting, the British, along with the Afghans, Danes, and Estonians, made steady progress towards the town. By the following day, ISAF forces had captured two villages south of Musa Qala and advanced to within two kilometres from its outskirts. By the end of the day, one British soldier had been killed when his vehicle was hit by a roadside bomb. ISAF commanders were now seeing success, but they needed more troops if they were to sustain progress – but few governments were prepared to send more soldiers to a conflict which had already cost hundreds of lives. ●

Chinook helicopters ferried supplies to support the coalition operation. (UK MoD)

CHAPTER FIVE

THE SURGE
MORE TROOPS TO AFGHANISTAN

Political pressure to send more troops to Afghanistan had been constant since the arrival of international troops in the country.

Commanders faced the dilemma of taking ground from the Taliban, but not being able to hold it because of a lack of soldiers. Then being forced to repeat the operation, after the insurgents had seeded back in to the region. Many countries were reluctant to increase their military contingents fearing casualties and the impact on public support. The challenge was particularly difficult in the south of Afghanistan where the Taliban now focussed the vanguard of its attacks on the coalition. Since arriving in Helmand in 2006, senior officers had constantly requested more resources in order to remove the Taliban and then reinforce that success; by holding the ground won from the insurgents, commanders could stop their movement. However, a cap on the number of UK troops in Afghanistan had been implemented by the then Labour government as it sought to avoid mission creep, particularly as British forces were still engaged in the campaign in Iraq. The consequent inability to control and own the

Political pressure to send more troops to Afghanistan had been constant since the arrival of international troops in the country. (DPL)

Coalition forces were now mounting major operations across the country to disrupt the enemy. (DPL)

deployed to Helmand in 2007 as a Joint Tactical Air Controller (JTAC), directing fixed wing ISAF jets who provided close air support to troops on the ground. Prior to his deployment, the then Chief of the General Staff (CGS), General Sir Richard Dannett, had called senior media representatives in to his office, from both print and broadcast, and agreed a deal of 'silence'. They all agreed that there would be no mention of him until he returned to Britain. The 'blackout' lasted just over two months. Then an Australian media agency was alerted to the news and posted on its website that HRH was in Helmand. On February 29, the Ministry of Defence confirmed that Prince Harry had left Afghanistan. The 23-year-old Prince had served ten weeks of a planned 14-week tour and was the first member of the royal family to serve on the frontline in a war zone since the Duke of York served as a helicopter pilot in the 1982 Falklands conflict.

battle space was thus having a negative impact on Task Force Helmand's progress, its casualties, and in meeting the strategic objective, namely the delivery of security and stability in the province. When President Obama took office in the US, plans for a surge were presented, but the new President took time to review the situation. In the meantime, Prince Harry had

Prince Harry had deployed to Helmand in 2007 as a Joint Tactical Air Controller (JTAC), directing fixed wing ISAF jets who provided close air support to troops on the ground. (UK MoD)

CHAPTER FIVE

Battle of Wanat

The insurgents campaign started anew in 2008 with an attack on a hotel in Kabul killing 100 people, which was followed by a series of attacks on coalition bases. The deadliest was in the east of the country and took place on July 13, 2008, in the Waygal Valley of Nuristan province – bordering Pakistan. The small village of Wanat lies high in the Hindu Kush at the southern edge of the province, in Afghanistan's rugged northeast. Jagged mountains, reaching as high as 25,000ft, tower over valleys that angle sharply down to winding rivers. Wanat was at the confluence of the Waygal River and a small tributary. It was home to about 50 families, who carved out a sparse existence on a series of green, irrigated terraces.

US airborne troops had established a temporary outpost in the village of Wanat to counter arms and ammunition being smuggled in from Pakistan. The base was listed as Combat Outpost (COP) Kahler in honour of First Lieutenant Matthew Kahler who had been killed earlier in the year. The soldiers were part of Chosen Company, 2nd Battalion, 503rd Parachute Infantry Regiment of the 173rd Airborne Brigade Combat Team. The COP was also established to provide security for the construction of a new road and to facilitate development projects in the region. The unit was part of Task Force Rock whose 173rd Airborne HQ was just five miles away. But despite being so close, the journey could take more than an hour along a road where ambushes and improvised explosives were common. The outpost sat at the bottom of a giant bowl which sheltered 'dead ground' – out of sight terrain – in which the enemy could

US airborne troops had established a temporary outpost in the village of Wanat. (DPL)

The remote base at Wanat was difficult for Chinook helicopters to access due to the high ground dominated by the enemy. (US DoD)

The terrain around Wanat was so mountainous that helicopters landed on small ledges to extract US troops. (US DoD)

hide. The battalion headquarters could not provide Wanat with steady, overhead visual surveillance because of adverse weather and limited availability of drones. The commander of the outpost, Lieutenant Jonathan Brostrom, was aware of the threat of a Taliban attack and had implemented a series of countermeasures. These included establishing observation posts and several defensive positions. However, the airborne soldiers had faced delays in the delivery of materials to build proper defensive positions due to the limited air support in their remote location.

The Battle of Wanat began in the early morning hours of July 13, 2008 when more than 200 Taliban insurgents launched a coordinated attack on Kahler. Here just 49 American soldiers and 24 Afghan National Army (ANA) soldiers manned the tiny base. The attackers used small arms, rocket-propelled grenades (RPGs), and mortars. The enemy infiltrated the village and moved dangerously close to the COP. But despite being outnumbered and facing an intense and sustained attack, the tiny airborne force mounted a blistering counterattack with small arms, machine guns and artillery support. They also called for air support from Apache helicopters and a B-1 bomber. The battle lasted for several hours. Lt Brostrom constantly directed his men and as they were injured, he ran to assist. At the height of the firefight, he was shot and died helping his men. As the smoke lifted in the sunrise nine American soldiers were listed as killed and 27 had been wounded.

A view from one of the machine gun bunkers constructed by the US airborne troops at Wanat. (US DoD)

CHAPTER FIVE

Wanat and similar areas were difficult to operate in, with villages often built into the side of mountains with narrow paths and little cover. (US DOD)

gunship could be heard above the convoy, ready to provide an immediate response if the enemy attack. On the ground a US special operations unit, Task Force 71, travelled on the flanks of the convoy ready to engage any Taliban. Ahead of the convoy an information campaign engaged with village elders. For three consecutive days, insurgents in the area of Kajaki were pounded by mortars and artillery, as well as being bombed by fast jets and attacked by Apache helicopters with Hellfire missiles. For the last phase of the route, the convoy had to turn on to Route 611, the main road between Nah-e-Saraj District and Kajaki and drive four miles through an area south of Kajaki where a 200 strong force of Taliban were known to be active. The enemy clearly knew the ground well and, with many very tight bends and

Kajaki Development

ISAF reinforced the British presence in Helmand with the deployment of the 24 Marine Expeditionary unit who had the task of clearing the Taliban from Garmsir in the south of Helmand. Meanwhile, the British were focused on the delivery of a turbine to the Kajaki Dam in the north of Helmand which would allow the hydroelectric facility to function at full capacity and literally 'light up' Helmand and supply power across the province and into Kandahar. In an operation codenamed Oqab Tsuka a convoy of 100 vehicles took five days to move massive sections of an electric turbine to Kajaki, covering 110 miles. The operation involved 2,000 British troops with 1,000 coalition soldiers from Australia, Canada, Denmark, and the US, as well as 1,000 Afghan troops. At night during the six-day operation, the familiar engine drone of a USAF AC-130 Spectre

US soldiers at Wanat after the battle in which nine American airborne troops died. (US DoD)

The Kajaki Dam in Helmand was the focus of a major development plan to install a turbine which would provide power across the region. (UK MoD)

In an operation codenamed Qoab Tsuka a convoy of 100 vehicles took five days to move massive sections of an electric turbine for the Kajaki Dam, covering 110 miles. (UK MoD)

high features overlooking the convoy's route, the risk of attack was high. It was the biggest logistical move by the British Army since World War Two.

More Troops

President Obama took office in January 2009 as insurgency in Afghanistan was on the rise. In February he approved the deployment of an additional 17,000 US troops to counter the violence. At the time, Washington had 36,000 personnel 'in country' while NATO nations had an additional 32,000. In April, the US commander of all forces in Afghanistan, General David McKiernan, was surprisingly replaced by General Stanley McChrystal, a former commander of US special forces. McChrystal reviewed operations and concluded a plan modelled on what was called 'courageous restraint' - instead of air strikes, fighter jets would fly low and fast to warn off the insurgents. The strategy also involved trying to persuade enemy fighters to defect and ultimately encouraging reconciliation between the Karzai government and Taliban leaders. Under McChrystal, US forces would protect the population from insurgents rather than simply kill large numbers of militants and train the Afghan Army to a level that they could take over security – this offered the US President an exit from Afghanistan. McChrystal was told to present President Obama with options, which he did. However, his three options all involved sending more troops to Afghanistan, which Obama was opposed to, and included: 10,000 additional troops to train the Afghan military and police, 40,000 additional troops to carry out a counterinsurgency operation and protect the population. This would raise the overall multi-national force level to 85,000 personnel.

Despite mounting pressure, Obama refused to commit to any course of action too quickly. Countless hours were spent reviewing strategic goals, questioning assumptions, and debating policy alternatives. The President eventually opted to send 30,000 additional troops.

On December 1, 2009, Obama announced his decision at West Point and implied that, given the stakes, he had appropriately matched means to ends, he said: "I have determined that it is in our vital national interest to send an additional 30,000 US troops to Afghanistan. After 18 months, our troops will begin to come home. These are the resources that we need to seize the initiative, while building the Afghan capacity that can allow for a responsible transition of our forces out of Afghanistan."

Battle of Wishtan

The surge of 30,000 US troops allowed ISAF to take the initiative and launch a major operation to provide security prior to the Afghan election in 2009. While the major offensive of the summer, Operation Panther's Claw, was launched a small British force maintained security in the village of Wisthan near Sangin. It was here in July 2009, that a foot patrol from C Company 2 Rifles, was to experience one of the bloodiest events of the campaign,

At night during the six-day operation, the familiar drone of a US Air Force AC-130 Spectre gunship could be heard above the Kajaki Dam convoy. (UK MoD)

CHAPTER FIVE

which would reveal bravery and courage above all expectation by extraordinary young men in extraordinary circumstances.

C Company had arrived at FOB Wisthan in late June to replace A Company which was taken out of the line to assist with the brigade's main effort, Panther's Claw, in which it was attached to the Light Dragoons.

Wishtan was in the eastern suburb of Sangin just minutes from the main base at FOB Jackson, with FOB Nolay a couple of miles to the south and FOB Inkerman – which had been named by Inkerman Company of the Grenadier Guards during their tour in 2007 - three miles to the north. In July 2009 there were no aerial surveillance balloons above the bases, which arrived later and eventually became common. These 'blimps' were fitted with cameras and electronic observation equipment which monitored the area and prevented the Taliban from planting IEDs and mounting attacks. However, in 2009, C Company did not have the benefit of such hi-tech support.

Devil's Playground

The local features of Wishtan included 'Pharmacy Road', the main thoroughfare, and a series of compounds that were surrounded by narrow alleyways and tree covered rat-runs which provided excellent cover for the enemy. Wishtan was an area of high tension, the Taliban regarded it as their territory and there had been numerous attacks on coalition troops. Almost every helicopter that flew into the base attracted enemy fire. Such was the level of kinetic activity that the soldiers of 2 Rifles often referred to the area as the 'Devil's playground'. On July 10, three sections of 9 Platoon, a total of approximately 30 soldiers, started the day with an early morning briefing, before preparing their equipment and moving out into the streets of Wisthan. Commanded by Lieutenant Alex Horsfall, the patrol set out

British paratroopers fought a bloody battle to remove the Taliban from Kajaki before the turbine arrived. (UK MoD)

Chinook helicopters flew troops ahead of the turbine convoy to secure the route and eject any insurgents. (UK MoD)

British troops used Javelin rockets to 'deny' Taliban forces access to the Kajaki area. (UK MoD)

The newly delivered Jackal vehicle, which looked like something out of a *Mad Max* film was now in service with UK forces. (UK MoD)

onto the dusty streets of the town at around 0430hrs. It was relatively cool - by noon, the daily temperature regularly exceeded 40°C. Heavily armed and wearing helmets and body armour the soldiers were confident, but as always very aware of the threat that could be waiting for them. The aim of the patrol was to familiarise incoming soldiers, who had arrived at the base to boost C Company's numbers. They would learn about local landmarks and be briefed about suspected insurgents in the area. The patrol headed for the local bazaar, which was already the scene of some early activity. During their pre-patrol briefing the riflemen had been made aware that a local man, living in a nearby wadi, was suspected of manufacturing IEDs. However, as they had no hard evidence of his involvement, all they could do was get the local Afghan Army commander to warn him that they were watching him. The enemy were cunning, they saw soldiers using ladders to scale the high

CHAPTER FIVE

The deployment of more US troops saw the arrival of a Marine Expeditionary unit in Helmand. (UK MoD)

the ground checking for IEDs. Known as the 'Vallon man', he literally held the lives of his colleagues in his hands. The Vallon had been a very successful item of equipment in locating explosive devices. But the Taliban constantly adapted their tactics, they knew the Vallon was a metal detector, so they started wrapping devices in heavy plastic. It was intense work for the 'Vallon man' as he took time to gently check the area in front of him. But nobody complained as his skill and patience saved lives.

In recent weeks, the number of IED finds had soared, as the riflemen maintained their methodical approach to clearing ground. Now, as 9 Platoon moved away from Wisthan, the slow progress allowed section commanders and soldiers to point out local features to those who had just arrived. As they headed for the local bazaar, the Vallon man held up his hand. He had found a device. The soldiers marked it and used another route. The increased spike in devices had overwhelmed the Explosive Ordnance Disposal (EOD) teams, there just

compound walls and avoid using doors which might be booby trapped so they responded by planting IEDs on top of the walls. They put devices into the walls and planted fake bombs in narrow alleyways to slow soldiers down. There had been a spate of incidents in the previous weeks in which insurgents had blown themselves up when planting IEDs. Now there was a concern that the Taliban only needed to get lucky with one roadside bomb, but in the meantime the riflemen were being extra vigilant.

The Vallon Man

Just days earlier the men of C Company had experienced their biggest attack since replacing A Company in Wisthan. The enemy had launched an assault from at least five positions with small arms and rocket propelled grenades, in what appeared to be a test of their defences. One soldier had been injured and evacuated by helicopter to Camp Bastion Meanwhile, as the morning patrol advanced the point man swept his 'Vallon' metal detector across

US Marines spearheaded the surge which President Obama agreed to prior to a withdrawal of US forces. (DPL)

The arrival of more US troops allowed commanders to reinforce their success. (DPL)

The surge also included more aviation assets which allowed the coalition to provide wider security (US DoD)

wasn't enough capability to deal with the devices and now soldiers simply marked the IEDs, leaving them to be dealt with at a later time. But very quickly the Vallon man found a second device, then another and then another. All their routes appeared to have been seeded with IEDs.

Lt Horsfall and 9 Platoon tried several more routes but on each one the Vallon man found potential IEDs. Lt Horsfall now opted to climb over a compound wall to evade the pathways and sent one section down a small valley and up the other side to some high ground, so they could provide overwatch. Suddenly there was an enormous explosion. An initial IED had gone off, then more detonated as a daisy chain of three or four devices blasted the patrol. This first explosion struck the command team leaving Lt Horsfall seriously injured. The incoming company commander was also injured, a section commander and a rifleman who was also a

Local Afghans wanted security but did not want to see more American and international troops in Afghanistan. (DPL)

Children were the innocent face of the Taliban – many of them acted as lookouts for the regime. (DPL)

section second-in-command had been hit, as well as the interpreter. Horsfall was in a bad way, he had lost his left leg and several fingers from his left hand as well as suffering injuries to his face. The blast had killed 18-year-old Rifleman James Blackhouse. Among the six injured was Rfn William Aldridge who had been hit by shrapnel. At just 18 years old he was the youngest soldier in 2 Rifles and had only been in Helmand for six weeks, having flown out from the unit's base in Northern Ireland to join the battalion in May. As the injured were being treated the Taliban opened fire adding to the chaos. Serjeant Jaime Moncho came forward to take command, overseeing the treatment of casualties and calmly making sure that despite the 'difficult situation' the young riflemen returning fire remained confident A radio message had been sent back to Wishtan informing the operations room that they had been hit. This message known as a 'contact report' alerted

CHAPTER FIVE

In Wishtan on July 10, 2009, a foot patrol from C Company 2 Rifles, was to experience one of the bloodiest events of the Afghan campaign. (DPL)

across pathways and narrow streets which they knew were seeded with IEDs. The ops room had called for the medical evacuation helicopter and a Chinook was quickly airborne from Camp Bastion along with an Apache escort and a Black Hawk from the US medical flight, known as Pedro.

The Vallon men from each section swept the compound for IEDs to make sure the Chinook could land safely. But as they swept the ground, they found more devices. The aircraft could not land. Instead, Sjt Moncho had to get the platoon back to Wisthan, where the landing site was secure. Just getting to the injured had been exhausting for the quick reaction force who had to clear their route of IEDs. Now the rescue team and the injured prepared to evacuate back to their base under heavy fire. Life saving treatment

the headquarters that they were under attack. More information quickly flowed regarding injuries. In the operations room at Wisthan soldiers listed the incident as a TIC or 'Troops in Contact' and deployed the Quick Reaction Force (QRF) with a quad-bike and trailer to recover the injured.

Blue Flash

Those who experienced the terror of an IED blast often spoke about a blue flash that sparked across the sky for a millisecond before an earth-shattering eruption. Often IEDs were packed with nuts and bolts as well as rotting animal remains in the aim that it would cause secondary infection to the wounded. The men of 9 Platoon were now taking cover and helping the injured inside a compound. Despite having been on the ground for more than an hour, the patrol was only 500 yards from Wisthan. The problem was getting back

Wishtan was an area of high tension, the Taliban regarded it as their territory and there had been numerous attacks on coalition troops. (DPL)

As they headed for the local bazaar in Wishtan, the 'Vallon man' held up his hand. He had found a device. The soldiers marked it and used another route (DPL)

had been given to Lt Horsfall who was in a critical condition and had been placed in the quad trailer. In what can only be described as 'courageous action', the soldiers fought back as they evacuated the seriously injured. Despite his injuries Rfn William Aldridge helped those more badly wounded. After the team medic carried out a tracheotomy on Lt Horsfall, he handed him over to Rfn Aldridge to monitor while he treated others. The quad and trailer headed the recovery back to base as enemy rounds continued to fly overhead. Then, as the four wheeled bike turned a corner a second blast ignited and was immediately followed by secondary blasts. The enemy had dug a huge bomb into a compound wall. Four soldiers received fatal injuries and others lay wounded. More troops had to come out from Wishtan to help, not having time to don body armour or helmets, so desperate were they to help their colleagues.

The enemy launched an assault from at least five positions with small arms and rocket propelled grenades, in what appeared to be a test of the FOB defences. (DPL)

Those who experienced the terror of an IED blast often spoke about a blue flash that sparked across the sky for a millisecond before an earth-shattering eruption. (DPL)

Eventually, of the 110 men who had been at the FOB that morning, only five remained at the base, four on the walls defending it, and one in the ops room, trying to coordinate the rescue effort and liaise with battalion headquarters at FOB Jackson. It took three helicopters to evacuate the casualties and the fatalities. Their names were added to a memorial at the base which was recovered when the US Marines moved into Sangin and replaced British troops in 2010. Those who died were Cpl Jonathan Horne, Rfn William Aldridge, Rfn James Blackhouse, Rfn Joseph Murphy, and Rfn Daniel Simpson. Five members of the patrol group, including their platoon commander suffered life-threatening injuries. It was one of the worst days in the history of the regiment and one of the least known stories of bravery during the war in Afghanistan. Sjt Moncho who had taken command of the situation was awarded the Conspicuous Gallantry Cross. ●

This first explosion struck the command team leaving Lieutenant Horsfall seriously injured. (DPL)

CHAPTER SIX
THE HUNT FOR BIN LADEN
OPERATION NEPTUNE

American special forces had been hunting bin Laden since the terrorist attacks on America in September, 2001. (US DoD)

In August 2010, US intelligence agencies received information which indicated that Osama bin Laden was living in a compound in northern Pakistan. The coalition was now reinforced with additional troops from the US and UK with a focus of hitting the Taliban hard in Helmand in a huge mission, codenamed Operation Mostarak and involving Canadian, British, and US forces.

At the same time America's most wanted high value target was now the subject of a top-secret plan. In the years since al-Qaeda had attacked America, the mission to find OBL had been a priority. The founder and former leader of al-Qaeda fled into hiding following the start of the war in Afghanistan fearing capture by United States or its allies. After evading capture at the Battle of Tora Bora in December 2001, his whereabouts became unclear, and various rumours about his health and role within the terrorist organisation circulated. Bin Laden also released a number of video and audio recordings, which appeared to taunt the coalition. But after a decade long hunt the Central Intelligence Agency was able to confirm that he was alive and living in Pakistan. They had located him by tracking one of his couriers, thanks to information gleaned from Guantánamo Bay detainees who gave the CIA the false name that the courier was using – Abu Ahmed al-Kuwaiti. In 2009, US officials discovered that al-Kuwaiti lived at Abbottabad in Pakistan and in August of the following year CIA operatives followed him back to the Abbottabad compound, which led them to conclude it was bin Laden's location.

Bin Laden had been hiding 'in plain sight' close to a military training college in Abbottabad just 160 miles across the Pakistan border. (US DoD)

World's Most Wanted

Since his escape from coalition forces, the exact whereabouts of the world's most wanted man had been at the top of the CIA's wish list. His state of health was a continuing topic of speculation. Weekly security meetings at the CIA's Langley headquarters focussed on OBL and routinely asked where was he hiding? Rumours were rife that bin Laden had been killed or fatally injured during US bombardments, most notably near Tora Bora, or that he had died of an illness. Reports also surfaced that he suffered from a kidney disorder requiring him to have access to advanced

Once it was known that he was living in Pakistan, the terrain in the region was studied by Chinook and Black Hawk helicopter teams. (DPL)

CHAPTER SIX

A scale model of the compound where bin Laden was living was produced by the CIA and used to plan the mission. (US DoD)

medical treatment, with further speculation that his second-in-command Ayman al-Zawahri had carried out the procedure. However, a CIA operator who had been in the Tora Bora mountains claimed that al-Qaeda prisoners there had confirmed that bin Laden had escaped to Pakistan. In June 2005 Taliban commander Mullah Akhtar Mohammad Osmani told Pakistani television interviewers that both bin Laden and Mullah Mohammed Omar were alive. He did not reveal anything about bin Laden's location, stating: "All I can tell you is that Osama bin Laden is alive and well." Then, in July 2009 the Pakistani Interior Minister Rehman Malik claimed that OBL was not in his country, adding if he was, the Pakistani authorities would know, and that bin Laden was in Afghanistan. A year later the then CIA director Leon Panetta told the media that the last time the CIA had precise information on bin Laden was 'the early 2000s'. Panetta added:

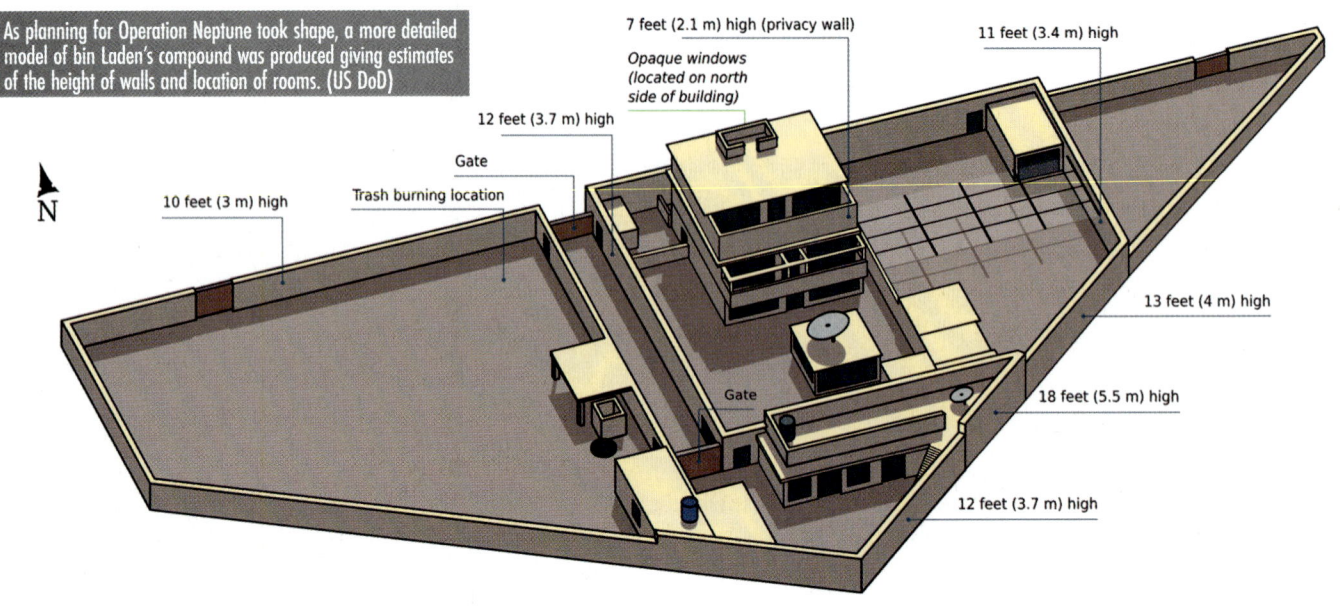

As planning for Operation Neptune took shape, a more detailed model of bin Laden's compound was produced giving estimates of the height of walls and location of rooms. (US DoD)

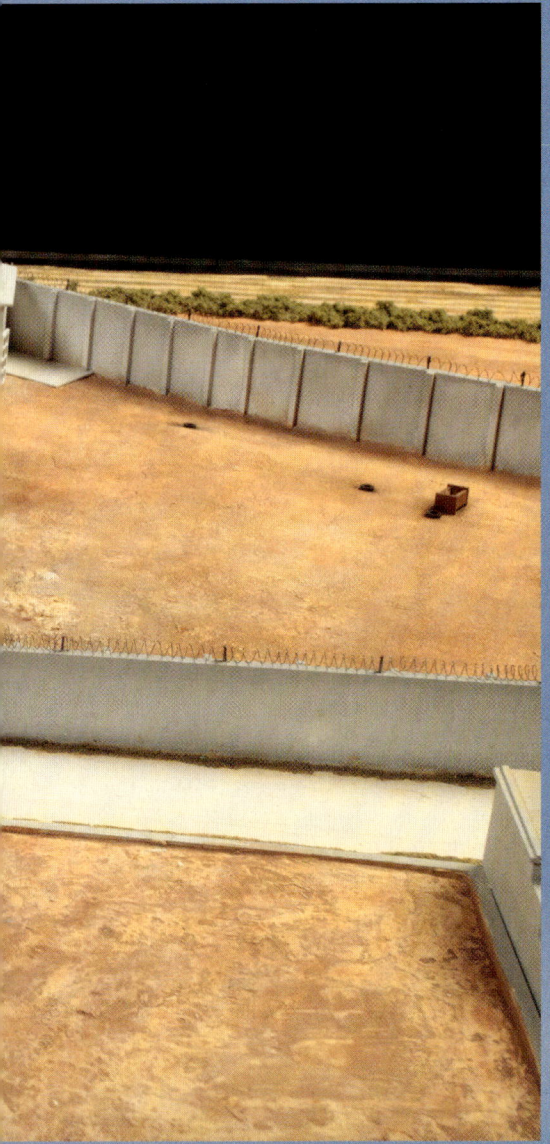

The evidence collected in the hunt for bin Laden resulted in Leon Panetta the head of the CIA seeking authority from the President to mount an operation. (US DoD)

"He is, as is obvious, in very deep hiding. He's in an area of the tribal areas of Pakistan, that is very difficult. The terrain is probably the most difficult in the world...All I can tell you is it's in the tribal areas...we know that he's located in that vicinity." His comments caused concern to those on the team hunting bin Laden, but Panetta was the head of the organisation.

Immediate Operations

Following the attacks of 9/11, the US Navy's SEAL teams were constantly on operations across Afghanistan and Iraq. Few were aware that these special units constantly trained for the call from higher command to kill or capture Osama bin Laden. Trained in counter-terrorism and hostage rescue, they had been involved in countless global operations across the Middle East and Syria. For almost a decade, American and coalition forces had followed bin Laden's footprints across the Tora Bora mountains and concluded that he was living in disguise in a nearby country.

Then, in early 2011 intelligence sources confirmed to US Special Operations that they had located the man who portrayed himself as the godfather of Islamic terror to a remote hideout in Pakistan. Sheltering in a heavily fortified compound at the village of Abbottabad, bin Laden clearly believed he was safe from capture.

Situated north of Islamabad, Pakistan's capital, Abbottabad is the 40th largest city in Pakistan. Abbottabad is in the foothills of the Pir Panjal mountain range and is popular in the summer with families seeking relief from the

Following the attacks of 9/11, the US Navy's SEAL teams were constantly on operations across Afghanistan and Iraq. (US DoD)

CHAPTER SIX

Obama spent weeks focussed on the operation and reviewing concerns about the US military flying into Pakistani air space. (US DoD)

blistering heat. Founded in 1853 by a British Army officer, named Major James Abbott, the city became the home of a prestigious military academy after the creation of Pakistan, in 1947. In 2011, the military college included elements of Pakistan's intelligence service and ironically was situated just a few miles from the home of bin Laden. High walls, razor wire and reinforced gates were designed to give him and his extended family permanent security. There were no mobile phones, no internet and communication with his cohorts was made by a trusted courier – the man US intelligence had monitored over months and identified as Abu Ahmed al-Kuwaiti. Even rubbish from the property was burnt to avoid any information being leaked about how many people were in the house or what they ate.

The unassuming property east of the Swat Valley was difficult to locate, it sat on the edge of the city attracting little interest from locals. It was estimated to be 150 miles from Jalalabad, which would be the nearest US base in Afghanistan for the SEALs to use as a forward mounting base. However, as more evidence came to light, commanders were confident that bin Laden was in the property and planned a raid to capture him.

The Location

Known locally as the 'Waziristan Mansion' the property that bin Laden had been hiding in was a large, upper-class house within a walled compound and had been acquired in early 2004. His trusted confidant (Ibrahim Saeed Ahmed) otherwise known as Abu Ahmed al-Kuwaiti paid a total of $48,000 to acquire a handful of adjoining small lots that together comprised roughly an acre in a soggy field just northeast of Abbottabad's city centre.

It still seems incredible that bin Laden was living almost 'in plain sight' of the Pakistani Military Academy for officers just 1,000 yards away. The refuge had been built between 2003 and 2005 as a three-storey mansion with its

Pilots from 160th SOAR planned a training route in the Arizona desert that replicated the flight from Jalalabad to Abbottabad and in the dead of night two Black Hawks and their SEAL team rehearsed the mission. (US DoD)

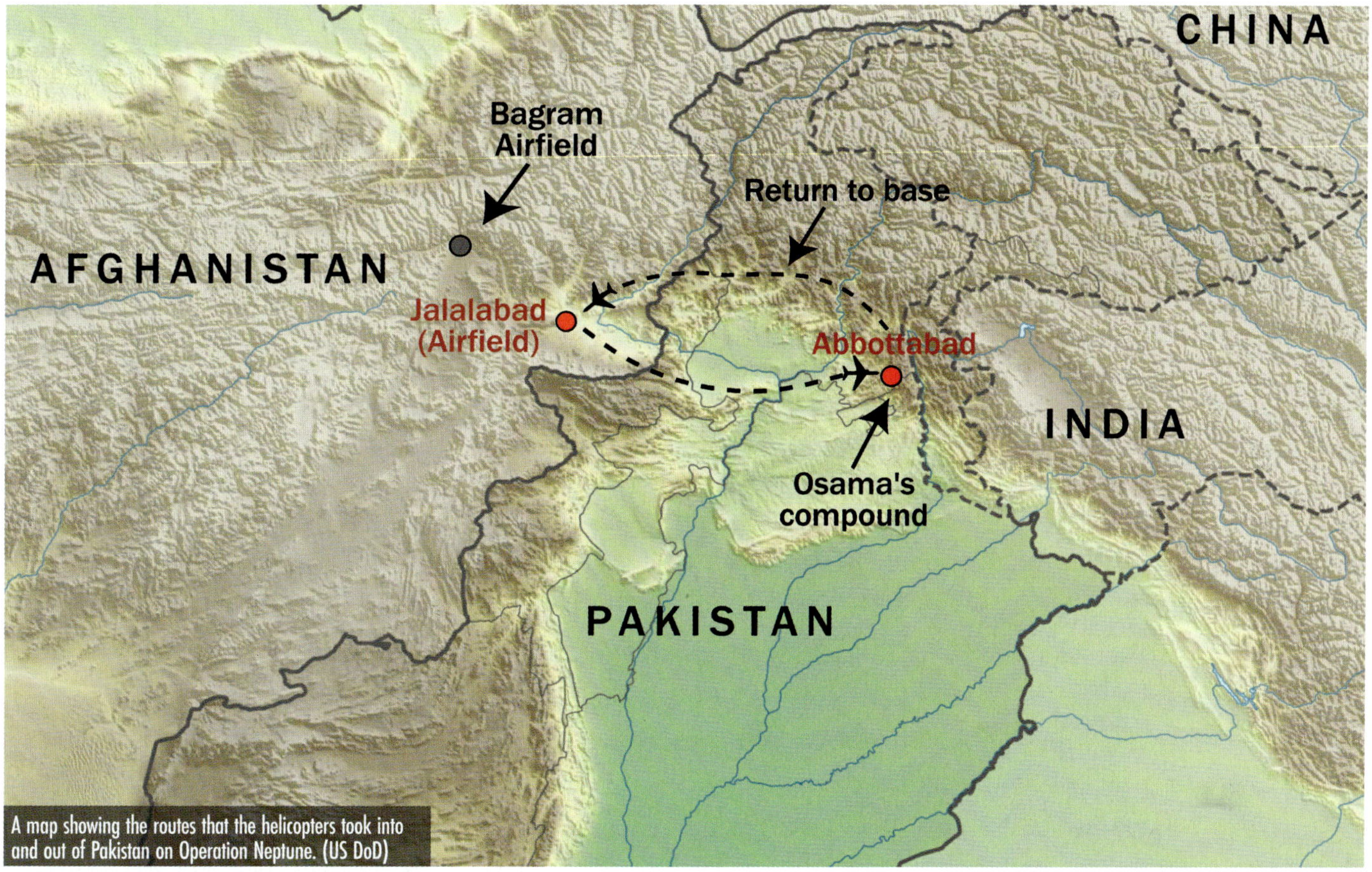

A map showing the routes that the helicopters took into and out of Pakistan on Operation Neptune. (US DoD)

own a compound, situated 2.5 miles northeast of the town. On a plot about eight times the size of nearby houses, it was surrounded by 12-18ft concrete walls topped with barbed wire. There were two security gates, and the third-floor balcony had a 7ft privacy wall. To identify the occupants of the compound, the CIA worked with doctor Shakil Afridi to organise a fake vaccination programme. Nurses attempted to gain entry to the residence to vaccinate the children and extract DNA, but security guards ushered them away. Surveillance of the property was managed by a special team of Pakistani CIA operators who knew the local customs and monitored the house by driving past in cars and vans. The courier was also closely followed when he went shopping into Abbottabad.

Life in the hideout was designed to be as self-contained and self-sufficient as possible to minimise contact with the outside world. The compound lacked telephone or Internet service – too easy to monitor - but did have satellite dishes allowing residents to watch the old televisions later found there. Bin Laden's son Khalid did much of the maintenance, and the compound had numerous animals including chickens, goats, and a cow.

The compound's inhabitants lived a basic life, there was no air conditioning in the hot summers and the lack of windows added to the warm air in the building. When the courier (Al Kuwaiti) headed to the local bazaars, he would stock up on naan bread, Coca-Cola, Pepsi, and sweets.

When SEAL Team Six raided the property, they found the compound stockpiled with medication. Bin Laden's computer included thousands of vital messages as well as popular Disney movies and American video games. Surprisingly, the vain terrorist leader even kept a stash of 'Just for Men' dye to mask the grey in his hair and beard.

Two of the rooms on the upper floors were used as bin Laden's media centre. On the back of a door, he hung the thobe (an Arab man's robe) that he donned when filming videos to be distributed to followers. A snub-nosed Kalashnikov, a memento from his days fighting Russian invaders in Afghanistan, rested on a shelf above the door. Yellow flowered curtains screened the room from curious eyes, and the walls were filled with hundreds of audio tapes carefully organised. Constantly aware of drones and satellites, bin Laden wore a large sun-hat when in the garden to ensure that any camera would not see his face.

Planning - Seal Team Six

SEAL Team Six was selected for the mission as part of a provisional contingency plan. Six is part of the Joint Special Operations Command, which in turn reports to US Special Operations Command, and conducts classified high-priority missions. Red Squadron within SEAL Team Six was chosen for the raid on Osama bin Laden's compound because it had just returned to the US from a deployment in Afghanistan and its operators were due to go on leave. It was therefore decided to extend their deployment in Afghanistan on paper as a cover for them to train without anyone asking questions about their preparations. At the same time, plans were being drawn to 're-engineer' two Black Hawk helicopters for the operation. The aim was to change the aircraft's shape and radar footprint so as to avoid Pakistani radar. In March, the head of US Special Operations Command, Admiral William McRaven, presented a plan to President

CHAPTER SIX

The compound in Abbottabad where bin Laden was hiding. (US DoD)

Black Hawk and Chinook pilots now moved to Afghanistan in readiness for the mission. (US DoD)

He gave his approval for the operation and SEAL Team Six was given the green light. Sat in Jalalabad the SEALs were 12 hours ahead of Washington and the news quickly came through that the mission was on. That evening at 10:30pm local time, 10.30am in Washington, the team took off from their FOB in eastern Afghanistan. Two 'special' Black Hawks carried 23 SEALs, an interpreter, and a combat dog as they lifted off towards the Swat Valley. An unarmed RQ-170 Sentinel drone flying more than 12,000 above Abbottabad transmitted a live video feed to the White House showing real-time footage of the target. In the situation room President Obama, his senior military commanders and principal advisors watched the raid play-out on a big screen.

Obama said he wanted to feel assured that the Americans could 'fight their way out of Pakistan' if needed and wanted support at Obama, but there was serious concern about transiting through Pakistan air space. Obama's advisors suggested an airstrike, but the military said that option was too dangerous and could kill innocent civilians. Robert Gates, the US secretary of defence, was firmly against the helicopter assault. He had been in the Situation Room at the White House when President Carter had agreed to the Teheran plan to rescue American hostages in 1980 - it resulted in a disastrous collision in the Iranian desert and Gates reminded the President that at the time senior military officials said all would go to plan. President Obama was now urged to bomb the compound, and the majority of his civilian advisors backed an airstrike by B-2 bombers. This would avoid any risk of US soldiers being killed or taken prisoner by Pakistani forces if the raid failed. However, Obama had faith in Admiral McRaven and directed him to start planning.

The President was concerned that bombing the target could result in civilian deaths and spark a major an international incident in which the United States would be condemned for bombing another country. In April, the SEALs 'development group' (DEVGRU) flew to a remote desert in the western United States. Pilots from 160th SOAR planned a training route that replicated the flight from Jalalabad to Abbottabad and in the dead of night two Black Hawks and their SEAL team rehearsed the mission.

The Operation

On March 14, 2011, President Obama met with his national security advisors. It was the first of five security meetings over the next six weeks. In the last days of April, President Obama was briefed for the final time in the diplomatic room where he authorised a raid of the Abbottabad compound. The government of Pakistan was not informed of this decision.

hand should anything go wrong. As part of the reaction force plan, four MH-47 Chinooks launched from the same runway in Jalalabad 45 minutes after the Black Hawks departed. Operated by the 160th Special Operations Aviation Regiment the MH-47 was ideally suited for the mission with its in-flight refuelling capability for long-range insertions.

Two of them flew to the border, staying on the Afghan side. Packed with a SEAL Quick Reaction Force (QRF) they would only fly in to Pakistani airspace if the assault force came under attack and needed support. The other two proceeded into Pakistan, each outfitted with a pair of M134 Miniguns. They followed the Black Hawks' initial flight path but landed at a predetermined point on a dry riverbed in a wide, unpopulated valley in northwest Pakistan. The nearest

AC 130 Hercules gunships were ready to support the operation if problems occurred. (US DoD)

As Obama gave his approval, a Reaper drone was launched high above the target. (US DoD)

AFGHANISTAN 69

CHAPTER SIX

Additional special forces troops flew in two MH-47 Chinooks who would follow the Black Hawks. (DPL)

house was half a mile away. On the ground, the copters' rotors were kept whirring while operatives monitored the surrounding hills for encroaching Pakistani helicopters or fighter jets. Arriving at the compound, one helicopter became unstable – possibly caught in winds – and forced a hard landing, leaving the aircraft damaged. The team of SEALs onboard was safe, and the mission continued. Most were armed with a silenced HK416 assault rifle as their primary weapon and a Sig Sauer P226 pistol on their chest. All carried a hydration bag, CamelBak or similar, some had energy gels, small packets packed with carbohydrates to boost endurance. Grenades and several magazines of ammunition were stowed in a combat chest vest. All wore personal radio systems

The picture showing the changed shape of the Black Hawks was released after the operations. (US DoD)

which allowed them to talk to each other, while a special medic carried a trauma kit, and an advanced communications operator carried a secure radio system to provide comms with Jalalabad. Inside the compound's walls, several SEALs approached an outhouse to eliminate any threat. The team found the door locked and were preparing to blow it open when a burst of gunfire came through the door. The SEALs returned fire. The door opened, and a woman came out carrying a child, followed by other children. Beyond her, lying dead, was her husband, Abu Ahmad al-Kuwaiti, bin Laden's closest aide.

In the main building, the SEAL team advanced, killing a second courier and his wife on the first floor and bin Laden's son, Khalid, who was armed, on the second-floor landing.

CHAPTER SIX

The Chinooks waited in rear of the advanced force with pilots flying on night vision systems and all navigational lights turned off. (US DoD)

As they moved in 'trained sequence', they followed their tactics of clearing each room before moving forward. They killed Osama bin Laden in his third-floor bedroom, he had at least one weapon nearby. With Osama bin Laden dead, the SEALs collected piles of documents, hard drives, electronics, and other materials for intelligence exploitation. And, as a backup helicopter arrived, they blew up the damaged Black Hawk to prevent Pakistani intelligence getting access to the aircraft's stealth technology.

Locals gathered outside the compound as several SEALs stood guard keeping them away from the house. Pakistani authorities began to mobilise a response to the late-night disturbance, but it was not clear what their reaction would be. Almost 45 minutes after arriving, the SEALs boarded the helicopters, taking with them the intelligence and bin Laden's body. Back in Jalalabad officers analysed bin Laden's DNA and took his fingerprints. Facial recognition analysis, together with the biometric information, which ultimately confirmed his identity. His body was then flown to the aircraft carrier USS *Carl Vinson* in the Arabian Sea. After religious funeral rites, Osama bin Laden was buried at sea so that his gravesite would not become a shrine for his followers.

Osama bin Laden is dead

President Obama went on television after the operation to announce that the United States had killed Osama bin laden. Speaking from the East Room, he said: "Tonight, I can report to the American people and to the world that the United States has conducted an operation that killed Osama bin Laden, the leader of al-Qaeda, and a terrorist who's responsible for the murder of thousands of innocent men, women, and children. Over the last 10 years, thanks to the tireless and heroic work of our military and our counterterrorism professionals, we've made great strides in that effort. We've disrupted terrorist attacks and strengthened our homeland defence. In Afghanistan, we removed the Taliban government, which had given bin Laden and al-Qaeda safe haven and support. And around the globe, we worked with our friends and allies to capture or kill scores of al-Qaeda terrorists, including several who were a part of the 9/11 plot. Yet Osama bin Laden avoided capture and escaped across the Afghan border into Pakistan. Meanwhile, al-Qaeda continued to operate from along that border and operate through its affiliates across the world. And so, shortly after taking office, I directed Leon Panetta, the director of the CIA, to make the killing or capture of bin Laden the top priority of our war against al-Qaeda, even as we continued our broader efforts to disrupt, dismantle, and defeat his network. Then, last August, after years of painstaking work by our intelligence community, I was briefed on a possible lead to bin Laden. It was far from certain, and it took many months to run this thread to ground. I met repeatedly with my national security team as we developed more information

President Obama and his team get word in the situation room that the mission has been successful. (US DoD)

about the possibility that we had located bin Laden hiding within a compound deep inside of Pakistan. And finally, last week, I determined that we had enough intelligence to take action and authorised an operation to get Osama bin Laden and bring him to justice. Today, at my direction, the United States launched a targeted operation against that compound in Abbottabad, Pakistan. A small team of Americans carried out the operation with extraordinary courage and capability. No Americans were harmed. They took care to avoid civilian casualties. After a firefight, they killed Osama bin Laden and took custody of his body."

The professionalism of the SEAL Team Six operation has never been fully appreciated – they flew 169 miles inside Pakistan, where they could have been intercepted and shot down by the country's fighter jets, then they mounted an assault into a heavily fortified building, and they still didn't know that OBL was there until they reached the third floor.

The Washington Post

MONDAY, MAY 2, 2011

U.S. forces kill Osama bin Laden; Obama: 'Justice has been done'

Decade-long hunt Death of terrorist leader marks the culmination of an intensive CIA effort.

In hiding Troops struck compound in Pakistan where bin Laden had been since the summer.

Jubilation Crowds gather to celebrate at Ground Zero and outside the White House.

BY BRADLEY GRAHAM

BY SCOTT WILSON AND CRAIG WHITLOCK

HISTORIC: Bin Laden's death will provide a clear moment of victory for Obama at a moment of deep turmoil overseas that is upending long-standing U.S. policy in much of the Muslim world.

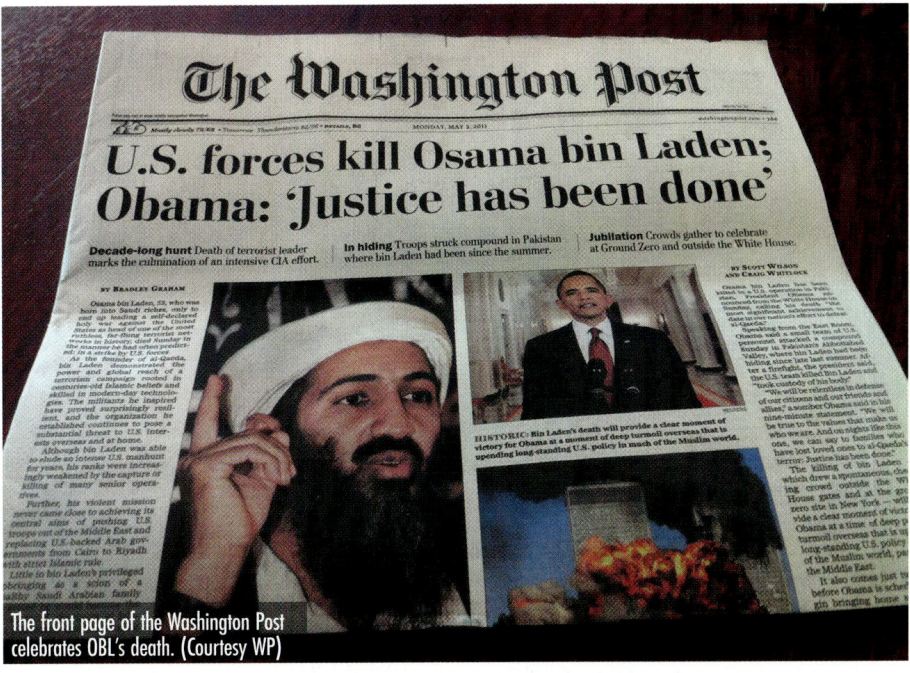

The front page of the Washington Post celebrates OBL's death. (Courtesy WP)

Tragedy in the Tangi Valley

On August 6, 2011, just weeks after the death of OBL, tragedy hit a US operation in Wardak province. A US Army Chinook, called Extortion 17, was shot down while transporting a quick reaction force who were attempting to reinforce a special operations unit of the 75th Ranger Regiment operating in the Tangi Valley southwest of Kabul. The resulting crash killed all 38 people on board, including 17 Navy SEALs, two UASF pararescue men, a US combat control team and seven members of the Afghan National Guard, as well as a dog handler and his animal and US crewmen from the USAF reserve and National Guard. The total loss of life was the biggest in the deployment of US forces, surpassing the loss of Turbine 33 which was shot down during an attempt to land a QRF in support of Operation Red Wings in June 2005. ●

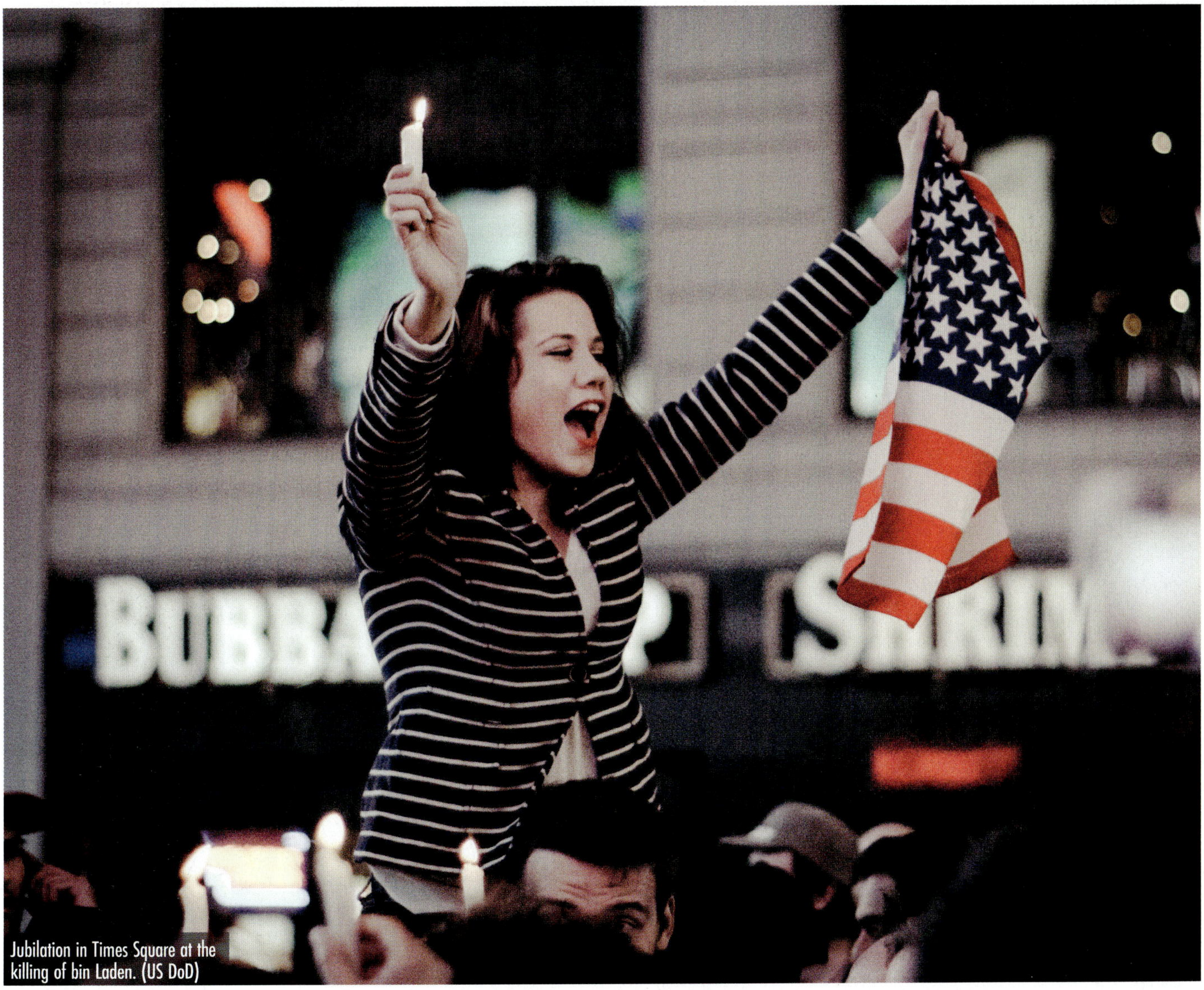

Jubilation in Times Square at the killing of bin Laden. (US DoD)

SUBSCRIBE TODAY!

Classic Military Vehicle is the best-selling publication in the UK dedicated to the coverage of all historic military vehicles.

from our online shop...
/collections/subscriptions

*Free 2nd class P&P on all UK & BFPO orders. Overseas charges apply.

CHAPTER SEVEN

Afghan National Army (ANA) cadets practice drills on the parade grounds at the Afghan National Defence University in Kabul, Afghanistan in 2013. (US DoD)

TRAINING THE AFGHAN NATIONAL ARMY

Since international troops first arrived in Afghanistan in 2002 and commenced a project to train and advise Afghan forces, the ability to deliver a well-trained, disciplined, and professional military had been a challenge. The importance of delivering a formed Afghan Army was seen as a priority to ensure that the government took control of its national defence policy and allowed international forces to leave. Within a couple of years, qualified Afghan recruits joined coalition troops on operations across the country. At first the relationship was strong, but the rapport quickly soured. The fact was that Afghans did not conform in any sense to the military culture of Western forces. While Afghan special forces were regarded as 'excellent', they were the exception. The majority of Afghan enlisted men appeared to regard service in the military as a requirement to earn money. Motivation and pride were in short supply, most likely due to the fact that many army units were crippled by corruption, drug taking, and desertion. Across

ISAF, international soldiers involved in the training of Afghan recruits reported that on operations Afghans deserted and sometimes refused to accept orders from commanders who were not from the same part of the country as them. This was not the case in all Afghan units, there were professional recruits, but they seemed to be in the minority. Interpreters were recruited and paid through a different system and assigned directly to coalition formations.

Trust was crippled when evidence surfaced that some Afghans were selling information to the Taliban about ISAF operations. Worse still, ISAF soldiers often avoided, where possible, working with the Afghans when the so called 'green on blue' attacks started in which Afghan soldiers turned their guns on those training them. The more educated Afghan personnel in the air force saw the opportunities for their country, but the army struggled to maintain a chain of command that accepted responsibility for the defence of Afghanistan.

Promotion was often shared among the more affluent Afghans which added to claims of corruption. The United States had spent $83bn training, equipping, and even funding the salaries of Afghanistan's security forces since 2001. They were gifted armoured protective vehicles, Black Hawk helicopters, and thousands of weapons. Time and time again commanders re-wrote the training manual for the country's forces, but when the ultimate test came in 2021, when the Taliban advanced on Kabul, the Afghan National Army collapsed and either surrendered to the Taliban or fled.

The International Trainers

Across Afghanistan, coalition forces embarked on various training projects to help the government deliver a well-trained Afghan Army. In the main they used AK47s assault rifles which were in plentiful supply as well as uniforms, boots, and personal equipment. In 2006 as part of their deployment to Helmand the UK military was charged with establishing a camp that would be used to 'train and assist' Afghans, as well as teaching them infantry skills. The British would then mentor their trained Afghan soldiers on operations against the Taliban. This concept was called the Operational Mentor and Liaison Team (OMLT) and involved a group of just five or six soldiers overseeing as many as 100 Afghans. Mentoring was not easy, many Afghans did not want to be in the army, they used drugs, and despite hygiene guidance from British troops they slept in the same uniform at night that they wore during the day and often for longer. In just a couple of months these British and international instructors, the unsung heroes of Helmand, had prepared and motivated the 3/205 Brigade to a level where in September 2006 an Afghan officer planned and directed, with UK assistance, the first major ANA operation into Garmsir in southern Helmand. It was designed to reinforce the town's district centre, after several hundred Taliban had threatened to overrun it.

However, as the operation progressed, a group of just 17 British troops escorting a 130-strong Afghan force, found themselves taking charge. The battle had commenced on September 11, the anniversary of the attack on the twin towers, and continued for six days. Outnumbered and short of food some of the Afghans were impressive, but soldiers said they needed constant support and needed to be motivated and told what to do. After their commander had been killed the Afghans stopped to pray and bury him – an act that allowed the Taliban to flee.

The first couple of years delivered thousands of trained soldiers at camps across the country and by 2008 the ANA listed 76,000 troops - a number that would swell to more than 150,000. Training was extensive and included specialist medical instruction as well as training for vehicle mechanics, bomb disposal operators, and engineers.

In 2013 there was still much optimism for the coalition-inspired Afghan National Army (ANA). Here cadets practice drills in the days before the Taliban retook control of the country. (US DoD)

CHAPTER SEVEN

Afghan Army Challenges

The creation of a new Afghan National Army was agreed at an international conference in Bonn, Germany in December 2002. At the conference, the new interim government of Afghanistan and participating donor nations agreed that the new Afghan Army (ANA) should be ethnically balanced, voluntary, and initially they suggested consisting of no more than 70,000 soldiers. The United States agreed to assume the lead role in the effort to reconstitute the ANA which would also include training for the police. Afghanistan's Army was divided into five Regional Commands (Corps) and was overseen by the Ministry of Defence and General Staff which were located in Kabul. The Regional Commands sat in Kabul (201st Corps), Gardez (203rd Corps), Kandahar (205th Corps), Heart (207th Corps), and Mazar-e Sharif (209th Corps). Recruiting was initially slow however and by June 2007, only the 201st and 205th corps were fully staffed.

A fully manned kandak, a battalion, contained 600 troops, meaning that a fully manned corps should have approximately 5,400 combat troops and 3,600 support troops. The ANA also faced challenges in terms of human resources, training, discipline, and professional relations, which was compounded by the absence of any chronicled, meaningful institutional record of the military. This history had simply not been retained and archived, despite the fact that the Afghan Army could be traced back to the 18th century. It had been reorganised in the 1880s during Emir Abdur Rahman Khan's reign and it had remained neutral during World War One and World War Two. And then from the 1960s to the early 1990s, the Afghan Army was equipped and influenced by the Soviet Union.

Afghan National Army Soldiers from 6th Kandak, 1st Brigade, 205th Hero Corps team with coalition counterparts during a patrol counterpart in Khanjegak village, Panjwa'i district, Kandahar province, Afghanistan. (US DoD)

Afghan National Army students on a tactical air coordinator course in 2014 wait to board an Mi-17 helicopter at Camp Shorabak, Helmand province, Afghanistan. (US DoD)

Recruitment of well qualified volunteers proved difficult as the ANA often attracted volunteers from the lowest areas of society. This caused problems in terms of education and literacy and even physical fitness. Illiteracy among the ANA rose from 60% in the 2002 to around 80% by December 2005. It was estimated that as of February 2006, approximately '50% of the officers of the army were illiterate'. This had an obvious negative impact on the ability of the ANA to operate jointly with US and ISAF forces and at the same time hindered the training process. The introduction of the Afghan National Army Officer Academy in 2013 raised this standard.

Communication problems existed not only between foreign trainers and Afghans, but also between the Afghans themselves, many of whom speak Dari or Pashto but not always both. In 2005 around 300 men simply walked away from the 205th Corps in Kandahar – desertion always remained troubling. Some estimates suggest that at any given time, between a quarter and a third of the strength of the average battalion would be 'absent without leave' (AWOL) and sometimes even more. The AWOL rate multiplied during Ramadan and winter, as troops preferred to be home with their families. Evidence and statements by ANA soldiers suggest that the primary reasons behind desertions and going AWOL included low pay, lack of equipment, low morale, an unwillingness to serve far from home, and a refusal to fight alongside foreigners against fellow Afghans.

This reasoning was compounded by the fact that until 2012, the monthly salary of trained recruits had been $80 which was poor when compared to the $200 that the Taliban offered for switching sides. Equipment was often sold to local militias and insurgents. There was also evidence that some ANA units were involved directly in the narcotics trade.

An Afghan National Army basic trainee sings the National Anthem before giving his oath of enlistment during a ceremony at the Gazi Training Center in Kabul on May 24, 2010. (US DoD)

AFGHANISTAN

CHAPTER SEVEN

An Afghan National Army soldier leaves for a partnered patrol with US Marines of Golf Company, 2nd Battalion, 7th Marine Regiment, Regimental Combat Team 7 at Forward Operating Base Sabit Qadam, Helmand province. (US DoD)

Afghan National Army Officer Academy

When British military operations ended in southern Afghanistan in 2014, UK forces remained in the country providing force protection in Kabul and training future Afghan Army officers at a base just outside Kabul called the Afghan National Army Officer Academy. After years of training and mentoring the army and police in Helmand, the training of Afghan officers was seen as a natural conclusion to the UK mission and the academy opened in 2013. The respected hallmark of British military doctrine and training was used as a benchmark to instruct future kandak commanders. Like the British Royal Military Academy at Sandhurst (RMAS) senior commanders viewed the Kabul college as the future jewel in the Afghan Army and a lasting legacy of military excellence. Based at Qargha, ten miles northwest of Kabul, the base looked like a huge university campus surrounded by snow-capped mountains. It was often referred to as 'Sandhurst in the sand'. Kabul was a hybrid establishment designed to meet the requirements of the Afghan Army and its historical traditions. Lectures on the Battle of Waterloo were replaced with lessons learnt from the Battle of Gandamak in the 19th Century where Afghan military forces wiped out a retreating British Army. ➲

Soldiers from 2nd Battalion, 503rd Infantry Regiment, 173rd Airborne Brigade, the Afghan National Army, and the Afghan border patrol conduct training on how to enter and exit a CH-47 Chinook. (US DoD)

Two Afghan and one coalition instructor from the Explosive Hazards Reduction Course (EHRC) speak with students about the lessons learned during a training exercise conducted on Camp Hero in southern Kandahar province. (US DoD)

The largest graduation ceremony of the Regional Corps Battle School recognises 1,400 Afghan students who completed the 215th Corps, Kandak training, aboard Camp Shorabak, Helmand province, Afghanistan. (US DoD)

US Army Soldiers, 2nd Battalion, 503rd Infantry Regiment, 173rd Airborne Brigade partnered with Afghan National Army soldiers and the Afghan Border Patrol conduct training on how to enter and exit a CH-47 Chinook helicopter in April, 2008. (US DoD)

An Afghan National Army (ANA) soldier, assigned to the 215th Corps, stands next to an ANA Humvee while guarding the Operational Coordination Center-Regional (OCC-R) during the Afghan presidential elections in 2014. (US DoD)

New recruits of the Afghan National Army line up to receive an issue of uniforms and equipment from US Army special forces soldiers in 2002. (US DoD)

CHAPTER SEVEN

The huge complex had been built by the US Corps of Engineers and designed on the Sandhurst model at a cost of £64m. Academic staff had their own facilities and the complex respected Islamic culture with praying areas, while male and female accommodation was separate. The British provided the overall structure for the training academy and developed a 'train the trainer' policy in which Afghans took a lead role in the delivery of instruction to the officer cadets. They were supported by officers from Australia, New Zealand, Norway, and Denmark who joined the mentor teams.

Afghan National Army commandos with the 1st Company, 6th Special Operations Kandak move to their target for an operation in Kabul province, Afghanistan. (US DoD)

A soldier with the Afghan National Army's 9th Commando Battalion (Kandak) speaks with a boy during a humanitarian assistance mission in the Herat district, Herat province in 2011. (US DoD)

In September 2013, more than 270 members of the first kandak, equivalent in size to two companies in a British Army battalion, arrived at ANAOA, having been selected from 10,000 applicants. Compared to the previous cohort of Afghan officers these candidates, from across the country, faced a selection board, similar to that for candidates to RMAS. It included an interview, command tacks, writing essays and a physical assessment. They were taught by Afghan platoon commanders and platoon sergeants, as well as being overseen and mentored by their British counterparts. Recruits spent 42 weeks at the ANAOA, over three terms, before graduating in September a year later. Although the training model was based on that used at Sandhurst, emphasis was placed on generating an Afghan ethos as the Afghan National Security Forces continued to develop. It was thought that the future security of Afghanistan was dependent on the professionalism and capability of its armed forces. ANAOA was therefore established to equip future Afghan military leaders with the skills they would require to meet this need.

During their time at ANAOA recruits were able to learn about leadership, engage in strategy and tactics, as well as military and

An Afghan National Army soldier with the 203rd Thunder Corps fires a 122mm howitzer during a live-fire exercise at Forward Operating Base Lightning, Afghanistan. (US DoD)

Afghan history – which had been revived into the syllabus to instil pride in the Afghan Army. Religious and cultural affairs, as well as physical education all played key roles in the training programme.

The academy had the capacity to train up to 1,350 male cadets a year, as well as 150 female officers. The aim was to create an institution that Afghans respected, but in 2021 it was abandoned as the Taliban took power and the site became home to the insurgents. Within weeks the classrooms were trashed and the buildings abandoned to the elements.

Green on Blue Attacks

The growing bond between Afghan and International forces was shattered when ANA soldiers – presumably in the pay of the insurgents – started to attack international troops who trained and worked with them. In October 2011 several off-duty ISAF soldiers were playing cards at a remote base in southern Kandahar. Suddenly a grenade exploded and shattered the stillness, followed seconds later by bursts of gunfire. Before any of the soldiers could raise a hand to defend themselves, one was dead from a bullet to the head, and a second was dying, shot three times in the back. They were not killed by the Taliban but were victims of a 'calculated and coordinated' attack by Afghan soldiers entrusted to work alongside their US colleagues. US Army Captains Joshua Lawrence and Drew Russell had been murdered by Afghan soldiers in a tactic which was quickly dubbed 'green on blue'. By April 2012 at least 63 coalition troops - mostly Americans - had been killed, and more than eight wounded in so-called insider attacks.

The attacks had started in 2009 with one of the worst incidents taking place in the Nad-e-Ali district of Helmand. A platoon of British soldiers had been mentoring the police at a checkpoint for almost two weeks and had just completed a patrol of the area when the shooting happened. As the soldiers relaxed, an Afghan policeman opened fire killing five British soldiers then the Afghans fled.

The flag of Afghanistan flies over the Afghan National Army on parade as British troops formally hand over the lead responsibility for security to Afghan forces in Lashkar Gah in July 2011. (US DoD)

On March 14, 2012, following a request by NATO defence ministers, the North Atlantic Council endorsed a plan to reduce the risk of attacks on ISAF by Afghan national security forces personnel. The plan was developed by the commander of ISAF in close cooperation with his Afghan counterparts. It was aimed at strengthening ISAF security measures; revising and improving vetting and monitoring procedures for Afghan national security forces; and intensifying cultural awareness training for both ISAF and ANSF to bridge the cultural gap. In cooperation with ISAF, the ANSF also undertook several initiatives to improve their recruitment. In addition, counter-infiltration staff were embedded with the ANSF and in training schools to monitor the behaviour of Afghan service members. But little changed, the attacks continued, and coalition forces implemented their own safeguards.

On operations they began to put the Afghans in the front so they could not shoot coalition troops in the back, in bases some units made the Afghans hand in their weapons and made the Afghans rest in separate areas. The damage was done and in camp or on operations Afghans were viewed with suspicion.

What went Wrong?

Western forces were convinced that training the Army National Army was the way forward to support the government, giving those involved in the nation's defence pride, it needed to help generate national unity.

However, after so much time and money had been invested in the Afghan forces, on August 15, 2001, the Taliban captured the Afghan capital and declared the war in Afghanistan over. The lightning speed with which the group made major territorial gains shocked many as the Afghan National Defence Security Forces – the army and police – retreated without putting up a fight.

After 20 years of military training and mentoring, teams from countries across the ➲

Afghan National Army soldiers, 4th Cannon Battery, 4th Combat Support Kandak, 4th Brigade, fire a 122mm D-30 towed howitzer during live-fire training at Multinational Base Tarin Kot, Uruzgan province, Afghanistan. (US DoD)

CHAPTER SEVEN

A British Soldier uses a model in the sand, March 29, 2010 to instruct trainers from the Afghan National Army 209th Corps how to deliver a set of orders during an operation. (UK MOD)

A British Member of the Kajaki Operational Mentoring Liaison Team discusses the local situation with a resident via a translator and ANA soldier during a patrol north of the Kajaki Dam in 2008. (UK MOD)

failed to see the corruption. Commanders were only interested in the number of recruits being trained and making sure the figures increased so that ISAF forces could depart – perhaps quite rightly because they had no command over the ANA. Instead, overweight, ageing Afghan commanders enjoyed a lavish lifestyle while private soldiers had little resources – many of them only issued with one uniform.

In the period 2006 to 2008 the drug taking, poor discipline and lack of pride within the ANSF was well known to ISAF forces, but as 2021 moved closer the condition and treatment of Afghan soldiers was ignored by Western commanders. Nobody questioned why the desertion rate was so high, and nobody proposed a pay rise to help retention. Hence, instead of fighting, the ANA preferred to save their lives by surrendering to the Taliban.

International politicians did not rate President Ashraf Ghani, he was seen as not being in control and failing to tackle the international alliance had seen Afghan security forces as both capable and professional. More than $83bn had been poured into train and equip the army, air force, and police. It may well have been that ISAF commanders preferred to look away, but corruption in Afghanistan's defence and interior ministries had been rife for many years. Ammunition and food deliveries were often 'lost' ending up in the Taliban's hands. ANA commanders embezzled money by submitting requests for salaries of non-existent 'ghost' soldiers. As this was happening, ANSF personnel were paid a pittance and refused time off to see their families, often for months - while commanders went home most weekends.

The ANSF had one of the highest desertion and casualty rates in the world. Facilities such as the 'train and assist' project in Kabul which operated to mentor and support the ANSF

Members of the Afghan National Army (ANA) search a road for improvised explosive devices (IEDs). (UK MOD)

ANA soldiers board a helicopter in 2018 as they mount their own operations supported by ISAF forces. (DPL)

and fight for his country. The Taliban's strategy of taking control of major border crossings, prevented Ghani's forces from reinforcing the Kabul. Many army units were cut off from the rest of the country and thus were forced to either flee across the border to neighbouring countries or dissolve. The complete collapse of the country's security reflected Ghani's loss of control. His forces had had everything, from helicopter gunships to heavy artillery, armoured vehicles, and the latest guns – but they simply did not have the will and the belief in their government and country to stand against the Taliban.

In the wake of the ANSF demise, a US paratrooper in Kabul for the evacuation said it was a great shame, he added: "The guys had all the equipment any army could ask for, to be crude, they had all the gear, but no idea." ●

problems his country faced – particularly in the area of security. The perception of many diplomats was that the President was losing command of his country. Rank and file soldiers did not trust their political leadership. No Afghan soldier was ready to fight and die to defend President Ashraf Ghani or the government. Conspiracy theories about a secret deal between the Afghan government and the Taliban were rife among Afghan troops. This environment of doubt and suspicion clearly undermined Afghan soldiers' resolve to resist the advance of the Taliban. Ghani also failed to deliver political leadership and was constantly re-appointing ministers - a sign perhaps that he was trying to curry favour with some. But constant changes to senior army and police positions undermined morale and performance. There was little 'unity of command' or leadership to take the country forward. Fundamentally, Ghani failed to deliver leadership – in fact when the Taliban entered Kabul he fled – despite claiming he would stand

As well as traditional military training, Afghanistan's soldiers received instruction in a wide series of trades. (DPL)

US soldiers oversee their Afghan counterparts during mortar instruction in 2013. (DPL)

CHAPTER EIGHT
END OF COMBAT OPERATIONS

In 2009, having approved the surge of additional US troops to Afghanistan President Obama said he wanted to see the goal of starting to withdraw American personnel by 2011. Then in early July 2010, the newly elected the UK Prime Minister David Cameron gave the first indication that he wanted all British forces withdrawn from Afghanistan by 2015. The Netherlands and Canada had announced already that they were withdrawing their troops in 2011, while Poland indicated that it planned to pull its forces out by 2012, three years before the anticipated withdrawal date of 2015. After five years of intense kinetic operations, British, American, and allied forces were now focused on an exit strategy, which was mapped out in a planned transition of responsibility

Despite political confirmation that forces were pulling out of southern Afghanistan, patrols to protect US, UK, and Afghan troops at Camp Bastion continued. (DPL)

and command to Afghan National Security Forces (ANSF). The handover was to take place alongside an ongoing programme of training and mentoring to develop the ANSF. This evolving plan aimed to deliver leadership skills, as well as artillery, engineering, and medical training.

Across Helmand, Afghan National Army (ANA) officers were being encouraged to take on more planning and command functions. The British operational area of responsibility was much reduced now that security at Musa Qaleh, Sangin, and Kajaki was under the control of US forces. President Obama's surge, in response to General Stanley McChrystal's security review, had seen the arrival of more than 20,000 US Marines in southern Afghanistan. The British area of operations was now centred around Lashkar Gah, with Nad-e-Ali, Nahr-e-Saraj, and Gereshk being

Afghan commanders were now planning and executing operation with coalition advisors in support. (DPL)

The Netherlands and Canada had already announced that they were withdrawing their troops in 2011, and the UK and US were now to end operations in the south. (UK MoD)

the main areas of responsibility. However, despite the reduction in the operational footprint, the task now was to manage a staged handover.

At the G8 summit conference in Canada, Prime Minister Cameron stated his desire to see troops home by the next general election in 2015. He said: "I want that to happen. We cannot be there for another five years having effectively been there for nine years already." Seeking to clarify Cameron's position the following day, the Armed Forces Minister, Nick Harvey MP, stated that the Prime Minister was 'not committing to a firm timeline' and that it would 'depend on the conditions on the ground.' In July, shortly before the Kabul Conference was due to be held, Cameron again stated in response to a parliamentary question that he did not see a combat role for British troops in Afghanistan beyond 2015. He said: "Let me be clear. Do I think we should be there, in a combat role or in significant numbers, in five

years time? No, I do not. This is the time to get the job done, and the plan that we have envisages our ensuring that we will not be in Afghanistan in 2015."

Preparing Afghan Security Forces

The start of 2012 saw the workload increase markedly for those units mentoring the Afghan National Security Forces (ANSF) to make sure that both the police and army were on track to take control of the region. While British forces planned and followed the path of transition, the insurgents attempted to undermine the progress and stability with a new wave of roadside bombs. Behind the scenes, preparations were now underway for the drawdown of the forward operating bases, many of which would be dismantled and their contents packed aboard trucks for delivery to Camp Bastion. Troops had endured six bloody summers and while commanders spoke of years of experience in Helmand, the reality was the British Army had endured

CHAPTER EIGHT

A Foxhound armoured vehicle supports a foot patrol near Lashkar Gah, commanders were now planning to hand this area over to the Afghans. (UK MoD)

security and stability within local communities by constructing and opening more schools, bazaars, and infrastructure remained a priority in order to grow confidence in the Afghan security forces. ANA officers were now learning about and conducting co-ordinated patrols, planning logistics and learning how to form and deploy their own counter-IED teams; for many of them, however, it was a huge learning curve.

The British concept known as 'train the trainer' had worked well, although there was still a lot to achieve. The ANA, for example, had plenty of drivers, but few mechanics who could maintain and repair vehicles. Throughout June, 2012, development projects, including new bridges, were completed. At Lashkar Gah, the Afghans had now been in control of the provincial capital for a year and progress was evident across it. A clear indicator that security was improving was the fact the Taliban had, in the past couple years, changed their tactics. In early 2007, after finding themselves overwhelmed in firefights on a number of

a collective six months, the length of an operational tour, multiplied by the length of the campaign. However, US forces, Britain's key partners in Afghanistan, claimed that six months gave the British time enough to deliver change, but that before they could reinforce that success they returned home. American commanders proposed greater continuity, and some specialist British officer appointments were now being extended to 12 months. Prior to Christmas 2011, the ANSF had taken control of security in Nad-e-Ali, but while the handover was going well, commanders were very aware that discreet mentoring and military support would still be required for a period after the transition of power.

In the meantime, Task Force Helmand units continued to oversee development projects and deploy routine framework patrols in conjunction with their Afghan counterparts across the region, as well as mounting 'intelligence led' deliberate missions against insurgents and their commanders. Building

Some bases were totally dismantled while others were passed to the Afghan National Army and manned by their soldiers. (UK MoD)

Despite the reduction in the operational footprint, the task now was to manage a staged handover. (UK MoD)

occasions, they had adopted the IED as their main weapon of choice. As security improved, however, more members of the civilian community were informing the Afghan police and ANA about the location of devices. Furthermore, with the huge US contribution in nearby Marjah, security and conditions in the areas around Lashkar Gah had improved greatly. This success for Afghan forces and ISAF had forced the Taliban to change tactics again, this time focusing on attacks by 'lone wolf' gunmen - Afghan National Army soldiers who turned their weapons on British troops. A number of measures had been taken to minimise the risk, but it was very difficult to monitor every Afghan working alongside them.

Courage on the Battlefield

In May 2012 the Grenadier Guards, commanded by Lieutenant Colonel James Bowder, had taken over from the Danish battlegroup at Nahr-e Saraj, west of Lashkar Gah, bolstering security and supporting the Afghan National Army in the wider transition plan. In June, members of the Grenadiers' reconnaissance platoon, commanded by Captain Michael Dobbin, were inserted by helicopter to engage an insurgent sniper team that had previously ambushed a British patrol, killing three soldiers, and had since been located by intelligence sources. It started as a routine operation for the guardsmen who as usual, before boarding the helicopter, followed all the usual procedures and drills that they had practised so often during training. Among them was Lance Corporal James Ashworth, a dedicated young guardsman who had previously served with the Guards Parachute Platoon. The platoon came under fire almost as soon as it left the helicopter, prompting LCpl Ashworth to lead his fire team in a charge over 300 metres to the heart of the enemy position in a nearby village where two platoon spotted an insurgent fleeing into a walled compound in the village. At that juncture, other Taliban insurgents entered the village to rescue their sniper team and engaged the platoon from several positions.

The immediate priority for Ashworth and his fire team was to flush the sniper from the compound in the village outbuilding. Accordingly, they split up, using grenades to clear all likely hiding places. Captain Davis was in the process of searching and clearing a corridor when the sniper emerged or, in Davis's words, 'popped out' and opened fire. 'I returned fire,' said Davis, 'and hit him in the stomach and hip.' Despite his wounds, the sniper succeeded in taking cover in a room from which, despite being trapped, he continued to put up a fight, responding with expletives to calls for him to surrender. At this stage, the situation reached an impasse. The use of a rocket launcher or an air strike having been ruled out, it was at that juncture that LCpl Ashworth volunteered to break the stalemate by throwing his last grenade into the room, enabling Capt Dobbin and Capt Davis to carry out an assault as soon as it exploded. Capt Michael Dobbin later said: 'LCpl Ashworth was killed while fighting his way through compounds; leading his fire team from the front, whilst trying to protect his men and he showed extraordinary courage to close on a determined enemy. For his outstanding courage LCpl Ashworth was awarded a posthumous Victoria Cross.

Camp Bastion Attack

In the first week of September, Prince Harry having previously spent three months on operations during early 2008 as a as a Joint Terminal Attack Controller (JTAC), returned to Afghanistan to begin an operational tour as an Apache helicopter pilot. He joined the Joint Aviation Group (JAG), which provided helicopter support to ISAF and Afghan forces operating throughout Regional Command (South West).

Based at Camp Bastion, his Army Air Corps unit, 662 Squadron, a component of 3 Regiment AAC, provided surveillance, deterrence and, when required, close combat attack capabilities as well as escort duties for other aircraft. Following an announcement by the Taliban that they would make the prince their top target, the Ministry

US operations remained constant so as not to allow the enemy to attack the forces who were preparing to leave. (US DoD)

The backloading of equipment and stores was huge and involved convoys crossing the desert bound for Camp Bastion. (UK MoD)

CHAPTER EIGHT

Engineering, recovery, and plant vehicles had to be driven across the open desert to Camp Bastion, often with Apache helicopter support overhead. (UK MoD)

A recovery vehicle at Forward Operating Base Shawqat is prepared for its journey back to Bastion and the UK. (UK MoD)

of Defence issued a statement about the prince's deployment, which said: "As with all operational deployments, Captain Wales's deployment has been long-planned and the threat to him and others around him thoroughly assessed. Any risk posed by Captain Wales's deployment, based on capability, opportunity, and intent of the insurgency, has been, and will continue to be, assessed, and has informed the decision to deploy him."

However, several weeks later, at 2200 hours on September 14, a group of 19 heavily armed insurgents dressed in US Army uniforms mounted a well planned and coordinated attack on perimeter defences, they split into three groups with one targeting guards in watchtowers while another opened fire on a group of US Marine mechanics before attacking aircraft refuelling stations and the base compound. The third group meanwhile attached explosive charges to a number of aircraft and fired rocket propelled grenades at others. A four-hour-long battle ensued in which the insurgents were killed or captured by US Marines and No. 51 Squadron RAF Regiment supported by an Army Air Corps Apache, a USMC Bell AH-1W Super Cobra attack helicopter, and armed UH-1 helicopters. Some of the USMC pilots and ground crew also took part in the battle, killing a group of five insurgents attempting to advance down the flight line area and a single insurgent who was in the process of trying to fire an RPG at the defenders. Hours later, a second group of insurgents was subsequently flushed out and killed by gunners of No. 51 Squadron and US Marines. Shortly afterwards, the final five surviving insurgents were observed near the flight line: four were killed by members of No. 51 Squadron and the hovering attack helicopters, while the fifth was wounded and taken prisoner. Two coalition personnel were killed and eight wounded in the attack, which resulted in six AV-8B Harrier IIs and a USAF C-130 transport being destroyed and two Harriers severely damaged.

US Marine Abrams tanks were deployed across Helmand to provide overwatch when the US military dismantled their bases. (UK MoD)

Transition to Afghan Command

By 2013 Afghan National Security Forces were leading and planning operations with UK mentoring staff in an overwatch role, offering assistance if required. Afghan forces were now being trained in Counter IED tactics, artillery drills, and combat medical care as well as the maintenance of vehicles to support their own operations. The Warthog vehicles of the Armoured Support Group were deployed across the region in support of the deployed company group. A wind of change was now blowing through Helmand. New schools and roads had been built, the ANSF were now on the brink of taking over complete responsibility for the province, having already taken control of security in the majority of areas, albeit with British forces shadowing operations. The Afghans continued to deliver framework security patrols and in January 2013 demonstrated their expanding capability by successfully launching a large and complex operation to build a bridge over the Nahr-e Saraj Canal, followed by a deliberate operation to locate a weapons cache. Forward operating bases, checkpoints and patrol bases were being handed over to the Afghans or closed by British forces, allowing their troops to withdraw to Camp Bastion. By June 2013 British forces held just 12 bases, including Camp Bastion, and plans for the handover in 2014 were now ahead of schedule. Likewise, the US were closing down locations amid concerns of a Taliban summer offensive in June and July. At Lashkar Gah, the lead responsibility for all areas of command was passed to the ANSF and elements of the Task Force Helmand headquarters at Lashkar Gah had already established a 'step up' command function at Camp Bastion in preparation for the main headquarters to leave the capital and fly forward to Camp Bastion.

Safeguarding the Transition

As the drawdown continued a security cordon was placed around the remaining UK troops. Lance Corporal Joshua Leakey

Prior to Christmas 2011, the ANSF had taken control of security in Nad-e-Ali and were being mentored to take on other areas. (US DoD)

CHAPTER EIGHT

Framework patrols continued throughout the transition as the enemy were clearly aware that coalition forces were planning to leave. (UK MoD)

Among the large equipment to be backloaded were armoured vehicles used to clear routes. (UK MoD)

with complete disregard for his own safety, dashed across a large area of barren hillside which was now being raked with machine gun fire. As he crested the the hill, the full severity of the situation became apparent: approximately 20 enemy had surrounded two friendly machine gun teams and a mortar section rendering their critical fire support ineffective. Undeterred by the very clear and present danger, Leakey moved down the forward slope of the hill, and gave first aid to the wounded officer. Despite being the most junior commander in the area, Leakey took control of the situation and initiated the casualty evacuation.

of the Parachute Regiment was deployed in Afghanistan as a member of a Task Force conducting operations to disrupt insurgent safe-havens and protect the main operating base in Helmand province during the transition The majority of operations took place in daylight in non-permissive areas, attracting significant risk.

On August 22, 2013, LCpl Leakey deployed on a combined UK/US assault led by the United States Marine Corps into a Taliban stronghold to disrupt a key insurgent group. After dismounting from their helicopters, the force came under accurate fire by machine gun and rocket propelled grenades resulting in the command group being pinned down on the exposed forward slope of a hill. The team attempted to extract from the killing zone for an hour, their efforts resulting in a USMC captain being shot and wounded and their communications being put out of action. LCpl Leakey, positioned on the lee of the hill, realised the seriousness of the situation and

The British BR90 vehicle which could lay a bridge across a river was among the biggest piece of the equipment that needed to be repatriated early. (UK MoD)

US Marines Abrams tanks were flown back to the United States by the USAF. (DPL)

Realising that the enemy still held the initiative, he set off back up the hill, still under enemy fire, to get one of the supressed machine guns into action. On reaching it, and with rounds impacting on the frame of the gun itself, he moved it to another position and began engaging the insurgents. This courageous action spurred those around him back into the fight; nonetheless, the weight of enemy fire continued. For the third time and with full knowledge of the dangers, LCpl Leakey exposed himself to enemy fire once more. Weighed down by over 60lb of equipment, he ran to the bottom of the hill, picked up the second machine gun and climbed back back up the hill again: a round trip of more than 200 metres on steep terrain. Drawing the majority of the enemy fire, and with rounds splashing around him, LCpl Leakey overcame his fatigue to re-site the gun and return fire. This proved to be the turning point. Inspired by Leakey's actions, and with a heavy weight of fire now at their disposal, the force began to fight back with renewed ferocity and regained the initiative, LCpl Leakey handed over the machine gun and led the extraction of the wounded officer.

Vehicles were cleaned, inspected, and then flown back to the UK and the US from Camp Bastion. (UK MoD)

CHAPTER EIGHT

A Husky armoured protected vehicle loaded aboard a C-17 at Camp Bastion. (UK MoD)

Operating Base (MOB) at Lashkar Gah and Patrol Base Lashkar Gah Durai were prepared for handover to the ANSF. A third base, MOB Price, would also be closed. From a peak of 137 bases used by UK and US forces, only Camp Bastion and Observation Post Sterga 2 remained under British control. All other main bases had been handed over to the ANSF, while those the Afghans did not require were dismantled. The ANSF were now leading 97% of all security operations across the country and carrying out over 90% of their own training. The hospital at Camp Bastion had been handed over to the US Marines while the British resources and staff were slowly drawn down. It had been a vital resource and the mortuary, named Rose Cottage, was now dismantled, and shipped back to Britain. Many wounded and injured had been given life-saving surgery and stabilised in the hospital before being flown home to Britain for further treatment. The Afghans

During the assault 11 insurgents were killed and four wounded, but the weight of enemy fire had effectively pinned down the command team. Displaying gritty leadership well above that expected of his rank, LCpl Leakey's actions single-handedly regained the initiative and prevented considerable loss of life, allowing a wounded US Marine officer to be evacuated. For this act of valour, LCpl Leakey was awarded the Victoria Cross.

End of operations

Afghan National Security Forces were now directing the operational tempo of operations across Helmand with liaison officers from Britain and the United States assisting both the Afghan National Army and the Afghan police forces. British troops still manned a limited number of bases and provided overwatch, but the deliberate major battlegroup operations were over. In January 2014, the Main

A Foxhound reversing into a C-17 transport aircraft. (UK MoD)

A Hercules C-130J transport plane lifts off from Camp Bastion ferrying stores out of the country. (DPL)

Soldiers carry out a forensic clean of an armoured vehicle before it was shipped back to the UK. (UK MoD)

into a fortress the size of the town of Bath. Its facilities included its own water bottling plant, three catering and mess hall facilities capable of feeding around 7,000 diners, a Pizza Hut, and a KFC. At its peak during the period 2011/12 it was home to 28,000 troops, including US and Afghan forces. Then, on October 27, 2014, the tactical withdrawal of hundreds of British troops from Camp Bastion took place. During the last hours before the base closed down, with British troops carefully watching for any insurgent activity, the watchtowers around Bastion's 40km-long perimeter wall were handed over to the ANSF one at a time. An official ceremony then took place to hand over the base formally to the ANSF. Its new Afghan commander, Major General Seyed Malook, said that he was sad to see his British friends leave after working with them for a number of years, but he was glad that were able to be returning home.

had established a hospital in nearby Camp Shorabak and had worked with ISAF medics for more than a year as British forces prepared to leave. The survival rate in the British-run hospital had been around 98%. Part of this had been due to the huge effort put in to speeding up the movement of coalition casualties from the injury point to the hospital in what became termed as the 'Golden Hour'. While ANA troops injured in Sangin faced an ambulance journey of up to six hours to reach the hospital at Shorabak, British soldiers would reach the hospital in a MERT helicopter, arriving literally within minutes of being wounded.

In April 2014, the British military headquarters in Afghanistan was formally absorbed into the wider US-led Regional Command (South West). UK command was now subordinated to the US, marking a further milestone in the plan for British forces to exit Helmand. Meanwhile, Camp Bastion was becoming smaller as time went on. It had been the largest operational British military base built since World War Two, growing

A final parade at Camp Bastion to hand the base over to Afghan forces. (UK MoD)

Soldiers head home as combat operations in southern Afghanistan come to an end. (UK MoD)

CHAPTER NINE

THE TALIBAN'S RESURGENCE

The Taliban's approach to the coalition intervention in Afghanistan was patient anger, they knew their time would come to seize power again and their attitude was that while the Westerners may have all the watches, they had all the time – the insurgents were in no rush. While the US led International Security Assistance Force (ISAF) mounted deliberate operations and destroyed Taliban operations across the country, the enemy had the ability to generate more volunteers in days from Pakistan. They would wait for days, weeks and used tactics to kill soldiers, while multi-national troops worked with a tight framework of rules. The resurgence of these Islamic extremists had first been directed by Mullah Mohammed Omar. The one-eyed former Mujahedeen fighter founded the Islamic States of Afghanistan in 1996 and headed the Taliban. He was was born in Kandahar and through the multi-national operation in Afghanistan he was constantly hunted by ISAF. The reclusive figure directed operations in southern Helmand with an iron fist, confident in the fact that one day, just like the Russians the US-led coalition would leave freeing the Taliban to seize power.

Mullah Omar was the man who had first steered the Taliban to power in Afghanistan by guile. Having won the hearts and minds of the population through religion he then

When in power before 2001 the Taliban had banned kite flying – one of Afghanistan's most popular pastimes – and maintained a strict form of Sharia law. (DPL)

obvious base for the insurgents. The province, the largest in the country, had easy smuggling routes to Iran in the west and Pakistan to the south and east. In 2001 ISAF had also paid limited attention to the south, it was close to lawless. The return to power would take a long time, but the Taliban and their cohorts were in no rush.

The Rise of the Taliban

With its institutions dismantled after the Soviet occupation, Afghanistan was totally lawless and could not protect or safeguard its

The Taliban's approach to the coalition intervention in Afghanistan was patient anger, they knew their time would come to seize power again. (DPL)

Prior to 2001, the Taliban mounted religious patrols in the main cities and punished any they believed were not honouring the Koran. (DPL)

stamped his authority on the country with an extreme form of Sharia law. Even in 2006 he was directing operations in Helmand and confident that he could guide the group back to power.

The Taliban are a predominantly Pashtun, Islamic fundamentalist group. Prior to 2001 the Taliban had imposed a harsh interpretation of Islamic law despite pledges to respect the rights of women and religious and ethnic minority communities. Meanwhile, as they have transitioned from an insurgent group to a functional government, the Taliban have struggled to provide Afghans with adequate food supplies and economic opportunities. After the US led invasion that toppled the original regime in 2001, the Taliban regrouped across the border in Pakistan and began to plan their resurgence which was initially focussed on generating small cells of dedicated fighters who would move back into Afghanistan and establish groups in Kabul and Kandahar which could attack ISAF forces while rebuilding their network of terror across the country. In the south, Helmand was an

After the departure of the Soviets, the capital was left in ruins with decaying tanks and war damaged buildings. (UK MoD)

AFGHANISTAN

CHAPTER NINE

Taliban 'police' beat women in Kandahar after they were found guilty by the men in black. (US DoD)

intervention in Kuwait was the ultimate insult to all Muslims and blamed the United States for what he claimed was the 'Westernisation of Islam'. He thus launched al-Qaeda on a campaign to inflict terror on America and all Western forces who had stepped on to Muslim soil. In 1992 the group mounted its first operation, carrying out a bombing of the Gold Mohur hotel in Aden where American troops had been staying while in transit to Somalia; fortunately, they left before the bomb exploded. A second hotel, the Aden Movenpick, was also targeted, but the bomb detonated prematurely, killing two Australian tourists. A year later, in 1993, al-Qaeda attacked the World Trade Centre in New York, parking a van packed with explosives in the basement car park. The blast killed six people and injured 1,000. By 1994

citizens. Tribal conflict and corruption within the ranks of newly appointed government officials was common and continued to delay economic progress. In the 1990s a new Islamic group emerged, comprising religious scholars who had studied at madrassas in Quetta, Pakistan, and dedicated their lives to an extreme form of Islam. Headed by Mullah Omar, these Talibs (scholars) later became known as the Taliban and it was reported that elements within the Pakistan government were encouraging Omar, who was keen to develop the Taliban as a political force, to move into Afghanistan. Its military intelligence service, the Inter-Service Intelligence (ISI), was seeking to gain influence inside southern Afghanistan in order to maintain stability along the border between the two countries, and to reduce the flow of refugees into Pakistan. The ISI's 'hand' in the Taliban's expansion is unclear, but the latter quickly broadened their following inside southern Afghanistan.

Welcomed by Afghans, the group enjoyed the goodwill of the local populace who were exhausted by the bullying and endemic corruption, as well as the brutality and incessant fighting that was common among the mujahedeen. The first Gulf War in 1991, triggered by Saddam Hussein's invasion of Kuwait, was a turning point for Osama bin Laden who claimed the United States-led

Northern Alliance fighters on the outskirts of Kabul before they drove into the city in 2021. (DPL)

The poppy had been a main source of income for the Taliban who controlled the export to Pakistan and the West in a business which generated US$ millions for the group. (DPL)

Despite the war damaged streets, Afghan salesmen were selling pots and cooking equipment within days of the liberation by the Northern Alliance. (DPL)

the Taliban had secured a strong footing in Kandahar, a city with a population of 495,000, which provided the group with significant support and a base for their operations.

Now Mullah Omar's strategy for the Taliban was to gain control of Kabul and the entire country. Having secured the support of much of the populace, they switched to using fear and intimidation to exercise control and take power by introducing and enforcing Sharia law. A mutual alliance was formed between al-Qaeda and the Taliban, broadening the powerbase of bin Laden's terrorist organisation and raising the profile of the Taliban.

In 1995, al-Qaeda carried out an attack in Saudi Arabia, killing five Americans and two Indian workers at a US-operated Saudi National Guard training base in Riyadh. Meanwhile, the Taliban were now rising fast and taking control of more provinces across southern Afghanistan, sweeping towards Kabul, they were heavily armed and ready for victory. Equipped with weapons from Pakistan and large quantities of ammunition left behind by the Soviets, they made their move in 1996 and launched an offensive on the capital. On September 27, 1996, the Taliban entered Kabul and seized

The main road through Kabul came to life within days of being liberated by the Northern Alliance. (US DoD)

AFGHANISTAN

CHAPTER NINE

An artist at work painting the scars of the city weeks after the liberation. (DPL)

President Karzai was brought back from exile to head the country. He was seen by the Taliban as a puppet of Western forces. (US DoD)

power, establishing the Islamic Emirate of Afghanistan. After seven years of civil war, they now controlled much of the country. Life in the country was heavily restricted under Sharia law, with music and dancing as well as kite flying, which was a national pastime, now banned. Women and girls were excluded from school and men were required to have a fist-size beard on the bottom of their chin and to wear their head hair short. They also had to wear a hat or head covering of some sort. Those who opposed the Taliban faced a court and, if found guilty, faced lethal punishment. A panel of scholars sat in judgment on a range of cases from theft to adultery. Those found guilty faced the public amputation of a limb, being stoned to death or otherwise executed in Kabul's sports stadium. Many Afghans, who had supported the arrival of this new group, now wanted their old life back. Meanwhile al-Qaeda, which had been watching the rise of the Taliban, now recruited more followers and looked for another opportunity to mount a major 'spectacular' attack against the United States.

It came in 1998 when bin Laden's terrorists bombed the American embassies in Nairobi, Kenya, and Dar es Salaam in Tanzania, killing more than 200 people and injuring over 5,000. The attack sparked international outrage, but also generated a considerable amount of support for al-Qaeda within some Islamic countries. In August 1998, President Clinton signed an Executive Order imposing sanctions against Osama bin Laden and al-Qaeda. The order gave US officials the power to block accounts and impose sanctions on any government, organisation, or person providing 'material assistance' to bin Laden's organisation.

At the beginning of 1999, mid-level US officials travelled to Saudi Arabia and a number of Persian Gulf countries to seek information about charities supporting al-Qaeda and to attempt to put pressure on governments allowing such charities to operate. However, they received little or no assistance. In January 2000, in a move designed to gain recognition

With the Taliban routed by the Northern Alliance, Afghan families go about their business in Kabul. (DPL)

NATO troops provided security in Kabul in the wake of the Taliban's demise. (DPL)

Empires'. The British previously fought three wars here, the most recent conflict being the fourth. The first in 1842 ended in humiliation and the second, from 1878-1881, recorded a defeat at Maiwand. The third was regarded by many as a success, ending with an armistice on August 8, 1919 and reaffirmation of the Durrand Line which in 1893 established the border between Pakistan and Afghanistan. The Soviets invaded in 1979, and they suffered greatly.

In the most recent conflict – the fourth for Britain – most analysts suggested that the US coalition campaign with all its technology and military might also ended in defeat. The biggest hurdle that soldiers who served in Afghanistan faced was the culture. Afghans are mentally and physically robust. If a child is born with a severe disability, it is often left to pass away on the basis that it will not be able to care for itself and in the case of boy will be incapable of earning a living. Culture in the 34 provinces, home to a diverse ethnic population of Pashtuns, Tajiks, Uzbeks, and Hazaras is paramount. This vast country borders Iran and Turkmenistan to the west, Pakistan to the south and east, as well as ➲

Within a few years Afghan elders were not happy with the presence of Western troops and support began to grow for the Taliban. (US DoD)

as the official government of Afghanistan, the Taliban recognised the rebel Muslim government in the southern Russian republic of Chechnya. This infuriated Moscow whose forces were involved in a vicious and long-running conflict with rebel Chechnyans. Eight months later in September, al-Qaeda attacked a US Navy guided missile destroyer, the USS *Cole*, which was moored in Aden harbour where it was being refuelled. In Afghanistan, meanwhile, remotely situated training camps were now being used to gather and train al-Qaeda fighters who had arrived from countries across the Middle East and pledged their commitment to Osama bin Laden and to take part in jihad against the United States. Many would subsequently be captured or killed by coalition forces, but a small group underwent special training for a mission that would culminate on September 11, 2001, its effect having far-reaching and long-term consequences across virtually the entire world.

Afghanistan

The biblical tranquillity of the Afghan landscape hides a history of conflict that stretches back to Alexander the Great and Genghis Khan, as well as a host of other invaders who fought and left their mark on the country. When US and British forces arrived, they discovered what many considered a 'country trapped in time'. Many young men and women could not read, electricity was infrequent and non-existent in some regions. Outside of the big cities there were few hardened roads, people lived in what Westerners would consider feudal conditions – houses built from clay and mud, no television, no running water, and the women cooked outside on a fire. There was no equality for women, the Taliban had enforced Sharia law and girls had little opportunity. Afghanistan has often been described as the 'graveyard of

Afghan soldiers and policemen were being infiltrated by the insurgents and building their campaign. (US DoD)

CHAPTER NINE

At key events the influence of the Taliban was evident and by 2018 it was clear talks were needed to help the Afghan government remain in control and they had to consider involving the Taliban. (UK DoD)

As violence flared the majority of Afghans just wanted peace, but the Taliban were now building their capability. (DPL)

When in office President Donald Trump made it clear he wanted US troops out of Afghanistan and so arranged peace talks. (US DoD)

Uzbekistan, Tajikistan, and China to the north. In the 1950s Afghan politicians embraced change in a developing Islamic society. Firstly, with the emancipation of women in 1959, which involved the abolition of the veil, and secondly in 1965 the granting to women of the right to vote. Economic agreements with the Soviet Union and the United States attracted outside investment to fund new roads and the reconstruction of Kabul Airport. The US Corps of Engineers was based in Lashkar Gah in the 1950s when it supported a major irrigation project in the region, which included the Kajaki Dam. During the 1970s political and social unrest flared up, culminating in a military coup in April 1978 in which the People's Democratic Party of Afghanistan (PDPA) took power in what was known as the Saur Revolution.

When the Soviets left in 1989 warlords returned to armed struggle and fought for regional power and any women's rights were assigned to history. Their tough lives and hardships ensured that they could fight without fear and carry out what many Westerners might think 'degrading acts of violence'. Many 'armchair generals' had predicted that Afghans could easily be bought – how wrong their comments would prove to be.

Taliban tactics

The tactics of the Taliban were extreme but highly effective. They had no empathy for humanity, if a person did not agree with their view or disobeyed their laws. Their sickening tactics included the execution of women, often carried out if the mother had allowed her children to read. The aim was to strike fear in the family and the community which would allow them to rule with utmost terror. In 2006 the insurgents mounted a series of major attacks on the British to evict them from Helmand. Mullah Omar made sure the fighters took cocaine so that they would not back down in the face of a firefight and when his men faced huge losses, he turned to a tactics that had proved devastating against the Amercians and their allies in Iraq – the roadside bomb. The Taliban quickly learned how to produce the devices using the most basic of materials. Explosives were packed around nails and bolts, sometimes smeared with animal faeces to cause additional medical trauma through infection. They watched troops' patrol patterns and planted devices on pathways, tracks, roads and compound walls. As time went on, they dug larger roadside bombs deep into the ground and wrapped the explosives in plastic to avoid detection, wiring them up to pressure plates or initiating them by remote control. IEDs were often linked to others in a 'daisy chain' trap, designed to catch troops in a secondary blast. The impact of the IED was 'a game changer', although at the time in 2007 few

Soldiers could not open fore unless they clearly saw a fighter with a weapon and in a situation that threatened life. Finally, in his ultimate tactic before going back to Pakistan, where he died in 2013, Mullah Omar is alleged to have pioneered the 'green on blue' insider shootings in which Afghan soldiers shot dead their coalition trainers.

The Resurgence to Power

By 2018 Abdul Ghani Baradar, the Taliban leader freed from jail in Pakistan along with Haibatullah Akhundzada the overall figurehead of the group began plotting the rise of the group to power. Both were aware that many countries had withdrawn their soldiers and that the UK Prime Minister had announced in 2010 that his forces would leave by 2014. President Obama

President Joe Biden ordered a review of the US troop withdrawal from Afghanistan and extended it to September 2021. (White House)

senior officers were prepared to admit that the IED gave the insurgents the initiative. The fact remained, however, that the Taliban had changed the dynamic of the fighting and for the first time they were 'shaping the battle space'.

Now British and ISAF forces were forced to adopt greater protection for troops. The insurgents then took their tactics a step further and introduced the suicide bomber who walked up to a patrol wearing a chest bomb, hidden under his clothes, which as he got close to the soldiers he would detonate.

By 2021, Afghan President Ashraf Ghani's government was increasingly struggling to maintain security. (US DoD)

had also announced that US forces would drawdown. Back in 2014 when the UK and US left Helmand, the Taliban were quick to seize Sangin, Musa Qaleh, and Now Zad. The ANA in these areas were said to be among the best trained in the country but they offered little resistance.

By 2020 it was evident that all the Taliban had to do was wait while the US decided exactly when they would leave. The decision by Washington to withdraw troops by September 11, 2021 acted as the political catalyst for other nations to follow. After 20 years of support to the Afghan government during which Western powers invested US$ billions in development aid, delivered democratic elections, trained

The peace talks took place in Doha, but the Afghan government was not included which caused friction. (US DoD)

CHAPTER NINE

By 2020 the Taliban were now poised to strike and waited for the opportunity to seize Kabul. (DPL)

soldiers had been killed by the time the last Western soldiers left Kabul airfield in 2021. Since the intervention in Afghanistan, ISAF's command structure had regularly suffered troop shortages. Unlike the operation in Iraq when many countries objected to the invasion, the deployment of military force to Afghanistan was seen as legitimate in the wake of the attacks on the United States. But many of their military contingents came with caveats as governments did not want the political backlash if soldiers were coming home in body bags. Some would not allow their soldiers to operate outside Kabul, others refused to let them serve in Helmand, with one country claiming its forces were held in high readiness reserve when in reality they never left their camp at Kandahar.

The lack of troop numbers resulted in the Taliban often having the freedom to move from province to province. In one example in Helmand in the south of the country, the British faced a huge challenge. Their area of operation was the biggest in Afghanistan and while the original number of 3,100 troops the country's security forces, and made the ultimate sacrifices in blood and treasure it was time to fully handover control.

The Taliban, armed and heavily equipped with Western weapons taken from the ANA drove into Kabul on August 15, 2021 aboard American armoured Humvees – again taken from the ANA. That afternoon, President Ashraf Ghani fled the capital city by helicopter to neighbouring Uzbekistan. Just days earlier, he had sworn never to leave and said that he would die before abandoning his people. With Ghani gone, the Taliban offensive, which had captured dozens of provincial capitals in the preceding weeks, accelerated and within hours, the insurgents were in Kabul, sat at Ghani's desk, their resurgence complete. For many this was a conflict in which Western troops fought with one hand tied behind their back. The war in Afghanistan had delivered a high bill in 'blood and treasure' – the financial figure to sustain the conflict across the country was close to $200m a day and more than 3,000 coalition

Equipped with US weapons they had seized from the Afghan National Army, in August 2021 the Taliban moved into Kabul. (DPL)

As Trump ordered a date for US troops to leave, Ghani wanted them to remain. (US DoD)

The Taliban advanced on Kandahar, one of the biggest regional bases of the Afghan National Army and captured their camp and equipment. (US DoD)

fighters rejected all aspects of conservative and peaceful Muslim rule. In 1998, Bin Laden's cohorts were accused of being behind the bombing of US embassies in Nairobi, which killed 247 and at Dar-es-Salem where ten died. In response the US Navy was directed to attack Afghanistan and Cruise missiles were launched at suspected al Qaeda training camps inside Afghanistan and at what was believed to be an al Qaeda chemical plant in Sudan. After the 9/11 attacks on the US, coalition forces deployed to Afghanistan and linked up with the Northern Alliance to launch an offensive to depose the Taliban. Within weeks both the Taliban and al Qaeda were on the run and quickly defeated. But many Taliban fighters fled south, heading for Helmand. The exit strategy announced in 2010 by the US and UK sent a clear signal to the Taliban that they had an opportunity to seize power again. Politically, Washington and London wanted to get out as quickly as they could and hand over security to the Afghan government.

had increased year on year, commanders had struggled to make progress. Operations would see a battle group, 1,200 – 1,600, soldiers, clear an area of Taliban in what was sometimes a week-long mission. But because of the lack of troops, they could take the ground but could not hold it. As a consequence, when a new brigade arrived in Helmand, they would have to mount another operation to clear the same area. The Taliban simply danced around on the side-lines and waited for their opportunity The Taliban's total intolerance of the non-Muslim world was symbolised by the demolition of the giant and ancient Buddhas carved out of cliffs at Bamiyan in 2001. Fighting broke out after the Soviets left as warlords fought for regional control. Warlords in the north of the country formed the Northern Alliance and fought the Taliban for control of their land. The prevailing chaos and huge number of refugees made the country the ideal base for Osama bin Laden's al Qaeda network. The former Saudi businessman gathered his exiled followers in Afghanistan as well as other militants from Yemen, the Sudan, and other countries. This new force of Taliban

Taliban troops arrive in Kabul in 2021 aboard an armoured Humvee. (DPL)

Herat also fell to the insurgents as the Taliban headed for Kabul. (US DoD)

AFGHANISTAN **105**

CHAPTER TEN

As word spread that the Taliban were heading into Kabul, people panicked and made for the airport. Within a day, thousands were stood waiting for a chance to leave. (DPL)

KABUL EVACUATION

In 2021 Kabul was the scene of the biggest evacuation since the Berlin airlift that followed World War Two as the Taliban marched on the city sparking fears of a bloodbath in the capital. More than 122,000 from forty-two countries were flown out of the city as the insurgents seized power. As they advanced on Kabul, Afghan National Security Forces had failed to defend their country and capitulated in the path of the Taliban. Over the previous year's many army and police units had been infiltrated by the insurgents and this may have been one factor that allowed the Taliban to achieve such a swift victory.

During his period in office President Obama had stated he wanted to see a troop reduction after the surge of US soldiers in 2009. Throughout 2019 and into 2020 the Taliban had increased their attacks in Kabul putting pressure on the Afghan President, who appeared incapable of implementing security. Then in 2020, the then US President Donald Trump gave the insurgents the signal they had been waiting for. He reduced the number of US troops in the country and announced that American troops would leave by early 2021. His administration had conducted talks with the Taliban in the Middle East and on February 28, 2020, the US-Taliban Agreement - known as the Doha Agreement - was signed. This historic negotiation stated that the NATO mission would be out of Afghanistan no later than May 1, 2021, leaving little time for 20-years' worth of stores and equipment to be back loaded to Europe and the US. In March at a meeting at Camp Resolute, the

US Marines stand guard at the airport perimeter as Afghans hoping for evacuation start to arrive. (US DoD)

NATO Headquarters in Kabul, the commander of all forces in Afghanistan, General Austin Scott Miller, directed his forces to deliver an exit-plan. This required 17,000 troops from across 29 nations and 20,000 contractors to leave. At the time it gave nations 14 months to pack up and head home.

As the year continued, Trump ordered a further series of drawdowns of US troops and by September the total number of American personnel in Afghanistan stood at 4,500. Increasingly the plan to remove all US and ISAF equipment by May 2021 was looking impossible, unless a decision was made to destroy it.

Kabul timeline

The challenge for coalition troops to leave Kabul and the remaining bases was huge; decades of stores, vehicles, and equipment had to be flown out within a small time-frame. The plan was to close the bases furthest west first and then initiate a domino effect of closing bases back towards Kabul. One of the final locations to close would be the US operated airbase at Bagram Airfield. This would enable the US and partner forces to use the base as a key hub for the return of huge volumes of

Within hours of the first sight of the Taliban approaching Kabul, thousands of Afghans flocked to the airport forcing the military to quickly erect a perimeter fence. (US DoD)

CHAPTER TEN

American marine commanders discuss how best to control the crowds and make sure they have food and water. (US DoD)

A US Marine rescues a small child which had been left alone and needed medical care. (US DoD)

A USAF airmen searches the bag of an Afghan woman and her child before they board a plane to the United States. (US DOD)

equipment, while the remainder would use Kabul. At the same time Italy would close their base at Herat while Germany announced they would withdraw their troops from Mazar-i-Sharif - both of which had been established for 20 years. The Turkish government was yet to declare when they would withdraw and hand back Hamid Karzai International Airport, which was the key base of their forces. In June 2020 a plan had been drawn up and distributed to all nations, contractors, and civilian agencies serving with the NATO force. They were directed to start to reduce their population and return all unnecessary equipment to their home country as soon as possible. In addition, bases were now identified and planned for closure. But the initial phase of the drawdown did not start well due to the complexity of the task and the sheer volume of equipment that was to leave. A new plan then saw a blend of disposal and giving stores away while moving into other bases over the horizon closer to Kabul and re-deploying people and equipment back home.

For the US, it was a mammoth task, using the entirety of US Central Command's assets to airlift equipment out of country. The Bulgarians, Romanians, and Georgians were able to rotate troops through Kandahar and Bagram to provide security. By December 2020, both Herat and Mazar-i-Sharif were well on the way to closing. In February 2021 planning was going well, there were 9,592 NATO and non-alliance troops in Afghanistan. But the Taliban were advancing across the country, although at this stage there was still no clear

Some of the first families and entitled persons to be evacuated board a C-17 plane. (US DoD)

indication they would move on Kabul. By late February only bases at Bagram, Kabul, and Hamid Karzai international airport remained. Locations across the country were now closed and those that remained open were in the process of handing over to Afghan forces. The footprint of the NATO mission was shrinking by the week.

After the US election, the change in administration and the arrival of President Joe Biden had initiated a review by Washington of the operational timelines for withdrawal from Afghanistan. When President Biden took office, he had reviewed the departure date and announced that the exit plan would be extended until September. Military planners now wanted to backload everything by August – they had four months to complete the task. What he termed 'the forever war' was to end, and the timeline was to change yet again. On April 14, 2021 Biden said the drawdown would begin May 1 and conclude by Sept 11, but he said it would not be a 'hasty rush to the exit', adding that the US would leave Afghanistan 'responsibly, deliberately, and safely'. The President added: "After consulting closely with our allies and partners, with our military leaders and intelligence personnel, with our diplomats and our development experts, with the Congress and the Vice President, as well as with Afghan President Ashraf Ghani, and many others around the world, I concluded that it's time to end America's longest war. It's time for American troops to come home. The plan has always been in together, out together, with our NATO allies and partners. We will be out of Afghanistan before we mark the 20th anniversary."

A C-130J military flight takes off from Kabul as the international evacuation operation gets underway. (US DoD)

Afghan Army collapses

Biden's announcement was the signal the Taliban had been waiting for to advance on Kabul. By the end of July 2021, any remaining UK military troops had left, and the command and control of the capital was now firmly in the grip of the Afghan Security Forces (ANSF). However, by the middle of July, it was clear the Afghan National Army (ANA) was collapsing as the insurgents swept across the southeast of the country. In total they had captured 64 districts from Afghan government control. This was a surprise and a disappointment to those who had trained the army and police. It appeared that Afghan forces had not attempted to stop the Taliban and allowed the insurgents to take their weapons and vehicles. Now armed with US weapons and equipment, the Taliban continued its onslaught. They tore up the agreement made in Doha and continued to attack Afghan government forces in their assault, which was clearly heading for Kabul. President Ashraf Ghani, who had been elected in 2014, seemed powerless to stop the insurgents, but he pledged to remain in Kabul. Just months before the fall of the city, the US intelligence community had estimated that it would take the Taliban at least 12 months to take the capital, adding that the ANA in the city was unlikely to capitulate. Ironically, the Taliban were moving at pace as province after province collapsed. From driving around in a battered fleet of Toyota Hilux's the insurgents now drove armoured Humvees and wore US military body armour and helmets.

The Evacuation Process

In early August 2021, the security situation changed dramatically as Washington and London monitored the Taliban's progress. By the second week of July only 600 American soldiers remained to secure the military side of the city's airport as well as at the US Embassy compound in the centre of the city. The Turkish government had agreed to provide security at the airport for a short period after all coalition forces departed Kabul and the majority of British and American contractors had also left the country, but thousands of foreign nationals, aid workers and former NATO employees remained.

Desertion in the ANA was now higher than ever as Afghan military commanders negotiated local truces with Taliban commanders. The insurgents now made their move and seized Lashkar Gah, the former headquarters of

CHAPTER TEN

American paratroopers stand guard at the edge of the Kabul Airport runway to stop Afghans trying to climb into the base. (US DoD)

A fortunate father and his daughters wait inside the airport for their flight out of Kabul. (US DoD)

chiefs to send three battalions of US Marines as well as the 82nd Airborne to bolster security at the international airport in Kabul and allow an airlift to begin.

In London, the UK government came to a similar conclusion and announced that 600 troops would deploy to assist in the airlift of UK nationals. On August 13, the UK Prime Minister approved the deployment of paratroopers to facilitate the evacuation of British personnel from the country. In reality, elements of the regiment were already on the ground and working alongside American and coalition forces to secure the airfield and develop a plan to evacuate thousands of 'entitled' civilians. The initial arrival of paratroopers included two infantry companies who secured the military area in the north of the airport, while the western area was manned by the US Marines and the eastern area by units from the 82nd Airborne Division.

UK planners had estimated that 5,000 people were expected to be evacuated and flown out by both US and British operations. They then headed for Kandahar, the country's second major city, and the strategically important town of Herat followed. Across the country more Afghan troops surrendered as the insurgents moved closer to Kabul.

There was now serious concern that foreign nationals could be in danger. The US and the UK along with many other countries advised their nationals to leave as soon as possible on commercial flights which were still operating. In the UK, the Ministry of Defence (MoD) monitored the situation alongside the Foreign, Commonwealth and Development Office (FCDO). Contingency plans to repatriate embassy staff and British nationals should the need arise to mount an evacuation were being reviewed. On August 12, President Biden agreed to recommendations from his military

A US soldier passes a military ration pack to a young child who needed food. (US DoD)

A British paratrooper monitors huge crowds desperate to get into the airport. (UK MoD)

President had fled. Roads around the airport were gridlocked as Afghan families fearing for their safety headed for the airport.

The arrival of a third company of UK paratroopers provided the additional manpower that allowed the British force to expand its operation to the southern side of the airfield. During the night of August 16, an evacuation staging centre was established at the Baron Hotel. This was situated just outside the airfield near the main access point, called Abbey Gate. The short road journey from the hotel to Abbey Gate was quickly named 'Route Leeds'. UK passport holders in and around Kabul were now advised to make their way to the Baron Hotel where their 'qualification to be evacuated' was checked before they were escorted across the road to the airfield for processing. The area immediately in front of the Baron Hotel was ➲

civilian charter aircraft which had continued to fly into Kabul. But as the Taliban moved closer to the city panic gripped the population. Within days commercial airlines suspended their flights and much of the Afghan establishment had abandoned their posts, there was no security, the government had stopped working and banks closed leaving people unable to access cash; the city was now lawless and in chaos.

Taliban enter Kabul

Late in the evening of August 14, the Taliban reached the outskirts of the city. Their arrival sparked the US government to initiate its embassy evacuation plan. Helicopters started shuttling diplomats, military personnel and US citizens from the Green Zone to Kabul Airport. The British government also ordered its diplomats and military liaison staff to leave. On the morning of August 15, the first Taliban fighters were spotted inside Kabul, prompting the Afghan President and other senior leaders to head to the airport and leave the country. His departure sent a wave of fear across the city. Within hours Kabul descended into mayhem after news that the

Hundreds of young men climbed the fence and tried to get aboard a US Air Force C-17. (UK MoD)

Afghans pack in to the back of an RAF plane bound for the Middle East and then a charter to the UK. (UK MoD)

CHAPTER TEN

UK and US troops manage crowds which as time went on became frustrated and increasingly desperate. (UK MoD)

A Danish soldier raises a card to try and ascertain if there are any Danish residents or qualified persons in the crowd. (US DoD)

British paratroopers and US marines assist a woman in the crowd that was suffering from heat exhaustion. (UK MoD)

identified as the 'Chevron.' It was a congested area packed with desperate Afghans who waited day and night hoping to escape. The area at Abbey Gate was so chaotic that barbed wire was laid across the road to try and hold back the crowds and extra troops were drafted in to manage the huge numbers of people hoping to be called forward. Every few hours paratroopers cleared the area in order to allow vehicles to ferry 'entitled persons' (EPs) from the hotel to Abbey Gate and once inside the airport they were taken to the passenger processing area.

Families were now arriving and sleeping in the street all night in the hope of getting a flight out. Many had fake documents – simply photocopied, but begged soldiers to process them. International troops passed out food and water to Afghans packed into an empty sewage canal near Abbey Gate, remaining vigilant in case of an attack. The panic and anxiety of the public was something the US and UK soldiers had no control over, people begged and pleaded to be saved while others passed their babies to soldiers in the hope they could have a better life. Intelligence assessments now warned that the threat of a terrorist attack was high. The alert focussed on a suicide attack and with the road around the airport packed it would be easy for a bomber to loiter.

As the US ordered more forces into Kabul to bolster security, the UK did the same. In the panic and confusion hundreds of Afghans climbed the walls of the airport. Once inside

Hundreds of evacuees who have qualified for a flight out of Kabul wait to board a flight. (US DoD)

the airfield, they tried to make their way onto the main runways preventing aircraft taking off or landing. US and Turkish troops were sent to try to clear the runway but not before dozens of young men had climbed aboard at least one USAF C-17. Both 2 PARA and the US Marines swept the runway and taxiways to clear the large crowds of civilians away from the aircraft and re-establish airport security.

Desperation

When dawn broke the Afghan civilians were still inside the airport and, more ominously, armed Taliban fighters had set up checkpoints around the perimeter. For most of the morning RAF and US transport aircraft circled over Kabul unable to land. US Apache helicopters now flew down the runway to scatter the crowds. By late afternoon a degree of order was restored. The airport was now surrounded by a mass of desperate Afghans, possibly as many as 80,000. Every road was packed with people, all trying to grab the attention of soldiers in a vain hope that they could convince them that they were 'entitled.'

American marines and British paratroopers stared down their former enemy confident in their capability to deliver lethal force if needed. But throughout they remained focussed on the task of maintaining security and processing the evacuation of civilians. The number of Afghans seeking to get out of Kabul increased daily. Families stood in line with nothing more than the clothes on their backs, many carrying children. At all times international soldiers remained alert to the constant threat of being attacked.

Soldiers helped families as the Taliban stood just metres away watching. The insurgents stood cradling their US Army M4 automatic rifles. Some wore body armour, new boots, and webbing all seized from the Afghan National Army. They looked nervous and one error of judgment could have sparked a firefight. More warnings were now being made about a suicide bomber which was the battlegroup's biggest concern.

On August 23, the UK Defence Secretary Ben Wallace announced that the British operation had 'hours not weeks' to complete its evacuations after the US announced its ➲

American marines maintain security as an increasingly hostile crowd of young men who had not been selected for evacuation try to gain entry to the airfield. (US DoD)

Warning of a terrorist attack were now very high, and the coalition force had increased its security and awareness. (US DoD)

AFGHANISTAN

CHAPTER TEN

A Phalanx machine gun was on standby at the airport ready to shoot down any incoming missiles. (DPL)

intention to withdraw on August 31. The UK government said it would request a delay of the US deadline to allow more flights to take place. At an emergency meeting of the G7 the then Prime Minister Boris Johnson requested an extension of the US deadline, backed by France, Germany, Italy, and Canada. The Taliban said it would not support any delay. On the same day, it was announced that a total of 6,631 people had been evacuated by the UK since the airhead in Kabul had been established.

In the extreme heat young soldiers directed crowds queueing to get into the airport, many of them vented their frustrations at the soldiers. The majority of junior soldiers who deployed to Kabul had not seen combat service in Afghanistan and the dynamic tempo of the operation tested their competence every day. Soldiers constantly cleared areas close to the airfield, but the space quickly filled again as Afghans refused to disperse. Huge numbers of civilians had opted to pack into the sewage canal where they stood in waste water. This created further concerns of a potential crushing incident as well as a target for any suicide attack.

In a move to reduce the crowd size and increase security against an attack a decision was made to build a protective corridor between the Baron Hotel and Abbey Gate. British military engineers requisitioned a number of abandoned JCBs around the airport and used discarded ISO shipping containers to build barricades. This protective wall quickly improved security and allowed soldiers to control the flow of people. As the operation entered its second week the RAF, along with the US and its allies, began surging transport aircraft to the Middle East to increase capacity. On August 24, the efficient processing of personnel allowed enough refugees into the airport to fill ten RAF flights. The UK government now stated the 'overwhelming majority' of people had been evacuated. At this point the figure was close to 15,000 people.

Suicide Attack

Coalition forces were now on high alert for an attack which intelligence briefings indicated would come from ISIS, the so-called Islamic State. On August 26, a suicide bomber moved into the area near the Abbey Gate and detonated a device that was to kill and cause serious injury to hundreds. The exact method of the bomber's entry to the airfield perimeter remains unknown. The person detonated the bomb at 1750hrs local time. For those near the blast it was unmistakeable. A blinding white flash, a millisecond of silence and then a huge detonation. Hundreds of Afghans, many of them women and children, were stood in the area of the explosion. The explosion killed 13 US personnel and more than 170 Afghans, as well as injuring an estimated 200, many seriously. It was the deadliest incident the capital had seen since the city was liberated from the Taliban in 2001.

With crowds of people packed into such a small area the injuries were traumatic. For senior soldiers who had served in Afghanistan and other areas the immediate fear was a secondary device, which the insurgents would detonate when coalition forces had been drawn to the area to assist the injured. The impact of the explosion had detonated CS gas canisters carried by the US personnel which quickly filled the air and added to the bloody chaos. On August 27, the Kabul mission entered its final stage and started to close. As part of the drawdown, the processing centre at the Baron Hotel was closed. This enabled troops to focus on evacuating the final batch of entitled persons and others who had been cleared and processed. In addition to the UK mission the wider international coalition force, which included the US, Australia, France, Sweden, Norway, Spain, Italy, Germany, New Zealand, India, South Korea, and Switzerland, ferried more than 122,000 people to safety. ●

A total of 13 US personnel died in the suicide blast in the closing hours of the evacuation operation. (US DoD)